D. J. ATKINSON

HOMOSEXUALS
IN THE
CHRISTIAN FELLOWSHIP

with a chapter by
A. W. Steinbeck

WILLIAM B. EERDMANS PUBLISHING COMPANY
GRAND RAPIDS, MICHIGAN

CONTENTS

Copyright © 1979 Atkinson, Steinbeck, Packer & Beckwith
First published 1979 by Latimer House, Oxford
This edition published 1981 through special arrangement
with Latimer House by Wm. B. Eerdmans Publishing Company,
255 Jefferson Ave. S.E., Grand Rapids, MI 49503

Library of Congress Cataloging in Publication Data

Atkinson, David John, 1943-
Homosexuals in the Christian fellowship.

1. Homosexuality and Christianity. I. Title.
BR115.H6A84 1981 261.8'3576 81-5491
ISBN 0-8028-1890-0 AACR2

FOREWORD

LATIMER House exists to make available biblically-based resources to help Anglicans judge between proposed alternatives on matters where there is disagreement and decisions have to be made. Its track record might suggest that its interests are limited to liturgy, church order and ecumenical relations, but that is not so. Reform, renewal and righteousness in the realms of personal faith and obedience no less than of the church's public order and policy belong to Latimer's House's concern, and the present Latimer Study, which the House's Theological Work Group urged Dr. Atkinson to write, demonstrates this. The avowed homosexuality of many folk today, both outside and within the Christian church, raises theological, ethical and pastoral problems on which the Church of England needs to clear its mind and focus its policy. At the time of writing, a report from the Board for Social Responsibility is expected. What Dr. Atkinson has written will help us in assessing the report, and I believe that it will help us in many other ways too. I am glad that my last act as chairman of the Latimer House Work Group should be to write this Foreword, commending for study what seems to me a most valuable treatment of a poignant and difficult subject.

J. I. PACKER

ACKNOWLEDGEMENT

Latimer House Theological Work Group express their grateful thanks to Dr. A. W. Steinbeck, M. D., Ph. D., F. R. C. P., F. R. A. C. P., Associate Professor of Medicine at the University of New South Wales, and Head of the Division of Endocrinology and Metabolism at the Prince of Wales and Prince Henry Hospitals, for his ready agreement to allow his paper to be reproduced in this Study; and also to the Editor of the Australian Journal of Christian Education in which the paper first appeared in Papers 59, September 1977.

PART 1: A CHANGING SCENE

1. THE QUESTIONS ARE DIFFERENT

E. M. FORSTER wrote his novel Maurice in 1913-14, affirming that homosexual love can be enobling and that any perversity in the matter lies with the society which persecutes those who love in this way. He wants to argue 'vehemently', he tells us, that 'perverts' ('an absurd word, because it assumes they were given a choice, but let's use it') are, like other men, 'good or bad ... their disproportionate tendency to badness ... being due to the criminal blindness of Society ... The man in my book is, roughly speaking, good, but Society nearly destroys him, he nearly slinks through his life furtive and afraid and burdened with a sense of sin.'[1]

The novel was not published until 1971, the year after Forster's death. However, in 1960, Forster disclosed that unless the Wolfenden Report (1957) became law, Maurice would probably have to remain in manuscript. 'We had not realised that what the public really loathes in homosexuality is not the thing itself but having to think about it. If it could be slipped into our minds unnoticed or legalised overnight by a decree in small print, there would be few protests. Unfortunately it can only be legalised by Parliament, and M.P.'s are obliged to think, or appear to think. Consequently the Wolfenden recommendations will be indefinitely rejected, police prosecutions will continue and Clive on the bench will continue to sentence Alec in the dock. Maurice may get off.'[2]

In fact, of course, the Wolfenden Report[3] became the basis for the 1967 Sexual Offences Act. The Report recommended that homosexual behaviour should not in any form be cognizable by law unless it infringed public order and decency, offended or injured the citizen or exploited or corrupted others (particularly the young and persons in special positions of dependence). The Report accepted the view that 'there exists in certain persons a homosexual propensity', in the light of which they recommended that 'homosexual behaviour between consenting adults in private should no longer be a criminal offence.'

It is not only in the area of criminal law however, that the question is different today from what it was for Forster in 1960. Since then there has been a flood of literature from medical, 'gay lib.', Christian and other sources, attempting to 'think about' the problems Maurice focusses so sensitively. If homosexuality is not a crime, is it a sin or an illness? Does it need treatment, punishment or recognition? Or, is it simply an alternative way of affirming natural sexuality? Specifically how has the Christian Church responded - how should it respond - to a life-style and behaviour pattern hitherto so strongly abhorred, the causes of which are not agreed (and in any case seem to be less relevant in much recent debate), and the physical expressions of which result in every range of response from disgust and revulsion, to a responsible attempt to try (with Maurice) 'to connect up and use all the fragments I was born with'.

We shall attempt to illustrate with selection from the vast literature on these questions, the changing picture of homosexuality. For some, though perhaps only a small minority, to be homosexual is no longer a secret, but is a matter for affirmation. Maurice's furtiveness, fear and burden of sin have been replaced by the headlines of a liberation crusade; for some. For many, though, the pain of Maurice is their pain, and the agony of loneliness is their main preoccupation. In medical and psychological terms, also, the questions are different. Increasingly in some quarters, the question of cure for a pathological condition is changing to the question of acceptance of an alternative life-style. Yet others offer counselling for an alteration of sexual proclivity. And to these changing questions, there is a wide variety of Christian response, often based on different understandings of the meaning of the Bible, or on a different approach to its relevance and authority for contemporary life.

A secret or an affirmation?;
One of the primary factors in the much more open discussion of homosexuality now than there was 15 years ago, and of the willingness (sometimes 'determination') of some homosexually inclined people to 'come out' and affirm their own sexual preferences, has been the emergence of various activist homosexual groups and liberation movements. Their two basic precepts seem to be[4] (i) that homosexuals are fully the equals of heterosexuals, and (ii) that homosexuality as a way of relating is in every way on a par with heterosexuality. The first precept is about personhood, and manifests itself in bids for equality in employment, civil rights, decent treatment, equality before the law and so on. The second is about lifestyle, and is a bid for the recognition of homosexual equality in the matter of sexual behaviour, and the freedom to enter a short or long term sexual relationship with another person of the same sex, analogous to heterosexual relationships and marriage.

This change has been widely documented and we select only a few authors as examples. In 1963 H. M. Ruitenbeek edited an anthology, The Problem of Homosexuality in Modern Society, which included essays by Sandor Rado examining an adaptational view of sexual behaviour, by Evelyn Hooker, concluding that on grounds of homosexuality alone the homosexual person need not be considered neurotic, and by Simone de Beauvoir, on Lesbianism. Most contributors viewed homosexuality in terms of its neurotic aspects, although some were already proposing that homosexuality should not be viewed as pathological - perhaps not even neurotic[5] By 1973, Ruitenbeek (in Homosexuality, a

5

changing picture[6]) finds his earlier work surprisingly conservative. He comments that whereas ten years ago, the homosexual question was dominated by a debate about causes, now the primary question is how the homosexual can integrate himself, and be acknowledged, as a full member of the community at large. There has been a significant shift from 'an intense and often guilt-ridden preoccupation with his homosexuality' to a 'preoccupation with the homosexual community and the issues which have presented themselves in that community.'[7] There has also been a growing desire among homosexually inclined people to discard false identities, and to admit to themselves and to families and friends that their homosexuality is an important force in their personal makeup, to deny which they believe is to deny themselves. Likewise, just as 15 years ago, it would have been almost inconceivable to think of any organised homosexual student movement, now Student GaySocs are active, and Gay Rights committees are making their voices heard. Homosexuality as an alternative lifestyle is increasingly accepted and championed.

On the other hand, D. J. West in Homosexuality Re-examined (1977), a fourth edition, revised and augmented, of his book Homosexuality first published in 1953, concludes that at present 'a homosexual orientation is still a considerable social handicap', and those wishing to lead an overtly homosexual style of life 'encounter many obstacles', leading in some cases to chronic stress.[8] Even if love relationships between members of the same sex were to become fully acceptable, West would not agree with an attitude of complete neutrality towards the development of sexual orientation. 'On the whole, being heterosexual enhances a person's prospects of personal happiness and social integration. Sexual non-conformity can reflect an individual's difficulty in relating to others or in integrating love and sex, and these problems cannot be blamed entirely upon the attitude of straight society'.[9]

Generally speaking, however, the organised Gay movements disagree with this assessment, and claim that homosexual activity should be held to fall within the normal range of human behaviour. Some go further, and identify the campaign for homosexual liberation as a political endeavour alongside other political ideals. Thus Don Milligan's The Politics of Homosexuality (1973)[10] refers to those who choose to adopt a homosexual lifestyle as a political act in protest against aspects of society such as the nuclear family structure, or patriarchy, or traditional sex roles, or capitalism, for example. Such a specific linking of the Homophile Movement with revolutionary political concerns is explicit in Guy Hocquenghem's Homosexual Desire (published in France 1972, English translation, 1978).[11] His essay is 'born of a specific conjecture of theoretical and political concerns', and by developing both Freudian and marxist categories, he seeks to analyse the 'paranoid' hostility to homosexuality that modern capitalist society reveals; he relates this to the role of the 'Oedipal family', and 'reproductive sexuality in modern capitalism', and explores the possibilities of anti-capitalist and anti-Oedipal (family) struggles which he believes the Gay

6

movement affords. In his introduction to this radical book, Jeffrey Weeks speaks of 'the idea of homosexuals taking control of their own identities, and in doing so rejecting the stigmatising labels of a hostile society, which poses a real challenge to bourgeois ideologies of familial and reproductive sexuality and male dominance'.[2] This highlights in a very important way the extent to which the homophile movements are not only concerned with the affirmation of the homosexual person but also with a rejection of the family structure as the basis of society. It is of interest that at an early Nationwide Festival of Light meeting in 1971, at which a speaker was heckled by members of a homosexual movement, the first shout was 'Death to the Family'.[3] It also raises the question as to the extent to which the acceptance of a homosexual life-style is a matter of personal choice, and therefore of personal morality.

Only a minority of overt homosexuals, however, identify with radical political movements. More widespread in Gay communities is the sense of release that an accepted and acceptable identity can be found within a community of likeminded people, which removes the devastation of loneliness, and the guilt of living with a false identity before an apparently hostile world.

A sickness or a natural alternative?
Especially since the Kinsey Reports (of 1948 and 1953),[4] the question of homosexuality has featured prominently in psychiatric and medical literature. Kinsey proposed a hetero sexual - homosexual rating scale between O (exclusively heterosexual with no homosexual tendencies) to 6 (exclusively homosexual).[5] The Report also indicated the then surprising information that of the total male population in USA 37% engaged in at least some overt homosexual experience to the point of orgasm between the start of adolescence and old age, and that 4% of all (white) males are exclusively homosexual (rating 6) throughout their lives after the onset of adolescence.[6] By 1976, it was still the view of "most psychiatrists" (cf. W. Linford Rees)[7] that no cure can be offered to complete homosexuals with a Kinsey rating of 6, though a great deal could be done to make the homosexual a happier and better adjusted person.

In 1954, the Institute for the Study and Treatment of Delinquency published The Problem of Homosexuality by Edward Glover. From the standpoint of clinical psychology, he distinguished[18] between the 'three main factors' responsible for the homosexual condition: (i) constitutional or innate factors (now increasingly disputed[19]); (ii) developmental factors operating in early childhood and again at puberty; (iii) immediate or precipitating factors promoting sexual tension, and encouraging a homo-sexual form of discharge. He says that 'homosexuality is either a natural deviation or a mental disorder'. He also quotes research from the Portman Clinic at that time: of 81 cases treated (74 with psycho therapy, 7 with hormones), 36 were cured, 21 still had homosexual urges but had 'achieved discretion or conscious control', 6 were

7

definitely unchanged. None of those who had been exclusively homo-sexual since adolescence had lost their homosexual impulses, compared with 51% of the 'bisexuals'.

The following year, the British Medical Association published a memorandum of evidence prepared by a special committee of the BMA Council, on Homosexuality and Prostitition. This distinguished between (i) 'essential' homosexuality – believing that the condition in some cases was demonstrably of genetic origin (a theory now largely refuted[20]), and (ii) 'acquired' homosexuality, marked for example, by the continuance into adult life of schoolboy or schoolgirl activity, "seduction, imitation, segregation of sexes, indulgence without responsibility, defective homes, 'cultural aspirations', depravity." One of the most significant aspects of the BMA Report is the inclusion of sections on 'Religious Approach to Treatment':

> Individuals cannot, of course, be 'dragooned' into a religious experience and pressure in this direction would defeat its own object. There should, however, be recognition of the fact that homosexuals can acquire a new direction in their lives through religious conversion, and opportunities should be available to them to discover for themselves a basis of life that proves a reality to many people.[21]

> A Senior Prison Medical Officer who is also a consulting psychiatrist informed the Committee that he found common to all types of homosexual an innate sense of inadquacy. He believes that 'if homosexuals can be brought into communion (not necessarily literally) with a fixed body of people such as one meets in the Christian community a very great step in overcoming their sense of inadequacy and inferiority will be taken.'[22]

While the BMA Report acknowledges that most of the material for its research was necessarily obtained from prisoners and those undergoing psychiatric treatment, it does nevertheless point to a significant possibility of change for those who seek it. A whole Appendix is devoted to the question of religious conversion. 14 case histories are presented, 8 of these falling into the 'early environmental' and 6 into the 'acquired' group. All 14 were totally released from the 'mastery' over them of their homosexual tendencies through religious conversion. The Report further concluded that a 'healthy moral climate' facilitates such change, the operative factor being the evidence of those people who 'have the released and purposeful quality of life'.[23]

That was 1955. In 1962 Albert Ellis in America published 'The Treatment of Fixed Homosexuality' as a chapter in Reason and Emotion in Psychotherapy.[24] His moral judgement is largely statistical ('Kinsey has shown...'), but his own studies lead to this comment:

Fixed homosexuals in our society are almost invariably

8

neurotic or psychotic... no so-called <u>normal</u> group of homosexuals is to be found anywhere.[25]

Psychotherapy is of distinct value in helping homosexuals become less emotionally disturbed, less homosexual and more creative.[26]

Since 'fixed homosexuality' is a learned reaction and, as such, can definitely be unlearned, the best answer to the question 'How may bisexual, homosexual and inverted individuals be helped to overcome their emotionally crippled state... is 'to have them reared in such a manner that they do not become homosexual deviants in the first place! The failure rate in treatment is largely because 'most fixed homosexuals have no great desire to change'.[27] However, in that 'homosexuality is a general personality problem rather than a specific sex issue', psychotherapy can be of great value particularly when directed at 'the self-defeating philosophies of life which invariably lie behind fixed homosexual behaviour'.[28]

The same year, but from the psychoanalytic rather than the behavioural side of psychological medicine, came the influential studies of Irving Bieber.[29] His <u>Homosexuality: A Psychoanalytic Study</u> represents systematic study of 106 male homosexuals and 100 male heterosexuals in analysis with members of the Society of Medical Psychoanalysts. The researchers concluded that their study provided 'convincing support' for the thesis of Sandor Rado, that a homosexual adaptation is a result of 'hidden but incapacitating fears of the opposite sex.'[30] They see the development of homosexuality in a person as a pathological alternative to the fears and inhibitions associated with heterosexuality. Bieber specifically disagrees with Kinsey's position on the question of pathology:

Kinsey <u>et. al</u>. did not regard homosexuality as pathologic, but rather as the expression of an inherent capacity for indiscriminate sexual response. In support of this assumption the authors referred to the high frequency of homosexual experiences in the preadolescence of American males. Thus an assumption of normalcy is based on the argument of frequency, though in fact frequency as a phenomenon is not necessarily related to absence of pathology.[31]

Kinsey had also believed that the personality disturbances associated with homosexuality derived from the expectation of adverse social reactions. Bieber found that such anxiety could not account for the many significant differences between homosexuals and heterosexuals in the people he and his co-workers analysed.[32]

Bieber says that his findings are 'optimistic guideposts' for homosexuals and for therapists. 'A heterosexual shift is a possibility for all homosexuals who are strongly motivated to change'. 'Homosexuals do not bypass heterosexual developmental phases and all remain potentially heterosexual'.[33] Bieber's position has been widely criticised, although in 1976 he still stood by his earlier conclusions which, he says, keep the options open for homosexuals in the way that the 'new myth that homosexuality is a normal variant of sexuality' does not.[34]

Whereas many psychiatric text books place homosexuality within 'sexual deviation'[35] 'sexual perversion'[36] or 'sexual disorders'[37] however, there has been considerable resentment within the Gay movement against being regarded as 'treatable'. Thus in 1973 Gay Information published Psychiatry and the Homosexual: A Brief Analysis of Oppression, dealing with the treatment of homosexuality by main stream psychiatry. And typical of many within the homophile movement are the comments quoted in H. M. Ruitenbeek Homosexuality, a Changing Picture (1973): 'It is clear that most homosexuals have no desire to convert to heterosexuality and would not do so even if such changes were made easy and sure.[38] 'We don't want anybody's acceptance. We've begun to stand up by ourselves'.[39] One of the points of dislike concerning psychiatric treatment is that much of the evidence for research is based on interviews with treatment-seeking homosexuals, who are said not to be typical ('Psychiatrists claim that all their homosexual patients are neurotic: they don't seem to notice that their heterosexual patients are neurotic too.'[40] Bieber, however, believes that several studies of non-patient homosexuals show essentially the same findings as his own.[41]

Another influential study from the viewpoint of psychoanalysis is that of C. W. Socarides The Overt Homosexual (1968).[42] Socarides argues that there is no innate, inborn or genetic factor in homosexuality, but that the choice of a sexual object is 'learned, acquired behaviour'. Furthermore 'the male-female design' which is taught and exemplified from birth is anatomically determined, and is part of the 'evolutionary development of man', such that it 'is perpetually maintained, and only overwhelming fear can disturb or divert it'.[43] He notes that homosexuals are often doubtful about attempts to change, and that it is not uncommon for homosexuals to warn any individual attempting treatment that any change could at best prove only superficial.[44] He does believe, however, that there is often a 'deep unconscious desire to alter what early environment has so cruelly forced upon them'.[45]

A substantial weight of psychological opinion would now disagree with the therapeutic stances of Bieber and Socarides, and proposes that the offer of therapy to help homosexuals change be stopped, and instead that therapists concentrate on improving the quality of their interpersonal relationships.[46] Thus in the decade between Ruitenbeek's two publications,

> a great deal has happened to our thinking about homosexuality. Regardless of Bieber, Socarides, Hatterer et. al. who still advocate the pathology concept vis a vis homosexuality, there are now increasing numbers of psychoanalysts and psychiatrists who strongly feel that homosexuality should be considered as just another form of sexual behaviour, another variety of

10

sexuality, if you will, and who indeed no longer view
heterosexuality as the preferred life-style.[47]

The last few years have also seen many publications on 'homophobia'
and on homosexual counselling services. In 1973, for example,
G. Weinberg wrote Society and the Healthy Homosexual described as
'a powerful and persuasive treatise on homophobia, defined as an
attitude of revulsion and anger towards all things homosexual.'[48] Also
in 1973, the Bedford Square press of the National Council of Social
Services published the Report of a 1970 Working Party: P. Righton (ed.)
Counselling Homosexuals. In 1976, Jack Babuscio's We Speak For
Ourselves appeared, which sought by wide use of case histories and
transcripts from counselling interviews at FRIEND (the national
counselling organisation linked with the Campaign For Homosexual
Equality), to give help from within a homosexual viewpoint to any who
are involved in sexual counselling. On the moral and religious aspects,
Babuscio views much of the biblical material as culturally conditioned
and therefore largely irrelevant to current debates. He gives detailed
information about the problems and questions homosexuals feel
themselves to have to face as 'citizens of a world in which institutions
are designed to meet the needs of a heterosexual majority'. In 1977,
D. Ferris wrote Homosexuality and the Social Services, published by
the National Council for Civil Liberties. Reviewing this in Counselling
News[49] Antony Grey (author of Christian Society and the Homosexual,
Oxford 1966, and a counsellor of the Albany Trust) agreed with that
author's view: 'Fundamental changes in dominant social attitudes are
required before homosexuals will be able to live and work in society
with the same freedom as heterosexuals.' Grey says that this book is
'required reading for all counsellors who wish to sensitise themselves to
the pressures put upon homosexual people even by the so-called caring
professions.'

Much, but by no means all, medical and psychological opinion has
thus shifted considerably from the majority verdict of 15 years ago that
homosexuality was a questionable and treatable condition to the view
which promotes and seeks to sustain in good health the homosexual
lifestyle as a 'natural alternative'. It is without doubt true as
Ruitenbeek notes[50] that this shift is in part a response to the pressure
from activist homosexual organisations. In this context, the recent
press headline 'Treatment for 2 weeks can aid homosexual' is somewhat
surprising.[51] The American sex researchers Masters and Johnson have
apparently reported after 10 years research that they conclude that
sexual preference is part of learned behaviour, and that most of the 67
homosexual men and women treated were 'able to achieve a long-standing
reversal of their homosexuality'.

The changes in these sociological and medico-psychological approaches
to the questions concerning homosexuality have been paralleled by, and
to some extent have contributed to, a divergence within the Christian
Church's approach to these questions.

The divergences in Christian approach

It is not disputed that virtually all Christian theologians until the last twentyfive years taught that homosexual behaviour is a disordered result of the Fall of mankind, and that homosexuality is a deviation from the pattern for human sexuality intended by the Creator. Tertullian[52] John Chrysostom[53] Augustine[54] all regard homosexual behaviour as being 'against nature'. Aquinas believed that homosexual acts were sins against nature, the most serious sins of lust except bestiality, and rejected the view that homosexual behaviour harms no-one because homosexual practices are always 'an injury done to the Creator'[55] Luther considered the prevalence and toleration of homosexual activity among the clergy 'as one of the worst symptoms of decay in the Church'[56] Likewise Calvin is very severe in his treatment of homosexuality, although – with Luther – stresses that homosexual practice is no more or less serious than fornication, adultery or other expressions of sin[57]

The modern Lutheran theologian Helmut Thielicke, although well aware of much recent psychological science, (because of which, perhaps his approach is very sympathetic and compassionate), likewise concludes that homosexual practice cannot be accepted, condoned or idealised. His chapter on 'The Problem of Homosexuality' in The Ethics of Sex[58] attempts to handle the questions 'without defaming the humanum of the person so conditioned'. 'It is true that the homosexual relationship is not a Christian form of encounter with our fellow man; it is nevertheless very certainly a search for the totality of the other human being.' Thielicke tries to expound what the 'person so constituted by fate' is to think of himself from the theological point of view.' He comments on the contemporary debate, and then continues with ethical analysis; concluding that

> The fundamental order of creation and the created determination
> of the two sexes make it appear justifiable to speak of homosexuality
> as a 'perversion' – in any case if we begin with the understanding
> that this term implies no moral depreciation whatsoever and that it
> is used purely theologically in the sense that homosexuality is in
> every case not in accord with the order of creation.....
> The predisposition itself, the homosexual potentiality as such, dare
> not be any more strongly depreciated than the status of existence
> which we all share as men in the disordered creation that exists
> since the Fall.....[59]

There are none the less possibilities of relative healing inherent in creation:

> Homosexuality cannot simply be put on the same level with the
> normal created order of the sexes, but... it is rather a habitual
> or actual distortion or depravation of it. It follows from this
> that the homosexual is called upon not to affirm his status
> a priori or to idealise it ... but rather regard and recognise his
> condition as something that is questionable[60]

12

Thielicke himself accepts the view that constitutional homosexuality is largely unsusceptible to medical or psychotherapeutic treatment, and so argues first for 'acceptance', and then that 'the homosexual has to realise his optimum potentialities on the basis of his irreversible situation... Christian pastoral care will have to be concerned primarily with helping the person to <u>sublimate</u> his homosexual urge.[61] The English translation of Thielicke's work appeared in 1964.

Now however, the Christian church is engaged in a wide-ranging review of its attitudes, and the uniformity of traditional opposition to homosexual behaviour is giving way to a diversity of opinion. It is not only that advances in medical and psychological sciences have reframed the questions to which the Church needs to address itself, nor only that Christians have been unclear whether to join or oppose movements for 'liberation'. Different theological approaches are pulling in different directions, and perhaps most significant of all, confusion about the interpretation of the Bible, or - when interpreted - about its relevance and authority have led to widespread divergence within contemporary Christian thinking.

By far the most significant Christian book of recent years on this subject is D. Sherwin Bailey's <u>Homosexuality and the Western Christian Tradition</u> (1955)[62] This book, it has been said, marks 'the beginning of diversity of Christian outlook'. It has also been credited with the 'beginning of the Church's attempts to come to terms with the facts of contemporary homosexual experience.'[63] The book has come in for severe criticism at various points (which we shall discuss more fully in a later chapter), but is still widely influential. Bailey seeks to examine the Biblical and ecclesiastical attitudes to homosexual practice. He distinguishes between genuine homosexuality as a condition (inversion), and 'perversion' which implies the engagement by heterosexuals in homosexual practices (a distinction which, since Kinsey, may be thought too simple). Bailey argues that there is no foundation for the prevalent belief that Genesis 19 and Judges 19 refer to homosexual sin. On the contrary, he believes, God punished the men of Sodom and Gibeah for breaching the rules of hospitality. The 'homosexual' conception of the sin of Sodom first appeared, he argues, in the second century BC among Palestinian rigorists, and seems to have been inspired by hatred of the Greek way of life. (see Appendix to chapter 5 of this <u>Study</u> by R. T. Beckwith). Bailey blames the traditional Christian hostility to all homosexual practice on the very profound effect the (wrong, he says) interpretation of the Sodom story had 'on the fears and imaginations of the Christian West'. Bailey further argues that the prohibitions against homosexual practice in Levitious are not relevant to our contemporary culture. Furthermore, the New Testament authors were unaware of the distinctions between inversion and perversion (says Bailey), so that while the Apostle's teaching (in Romans 1, for example), gives decisive Biblical authority for censuring the conduct of those 'whom we may describe as perverts'[64], the New Testament can hardly be said to speak to the expressions of affection which may take place between 'genuine

13

inverts.[65,] These themes, among others in Bailey's important book, are now common currency in the Christian homophile movement.

It would be an oversimplification, however, to describe the divergences in Christian thinking only in terms of those who accept the main conclusions of Sherwin Bailey's 'ground-breaking study', and those who continue to affirm the traditional Christian view of the homosexual condition as questionable and homosexual acts as sinful. At least three main streams of Christian thinking may be illustrated from recent literature, although the dividing lines between even these categories is not always clear cut. There have been Christian writings which, with varying degrees of understanding of modern psychological insights, have maintained the traditional interpretation of the Bible, affirming homosexual behaviour as being contrary to the will of God, and as regarding that interpretation as decisive for Christian morality today. There have been some writers who have tried to develop a mediating position, recognising the tragic and questionable nature of the homosexual condition, but believing also that in that non-ideal situation, Christian morality can find room for some homosexual behaviour as being permissible. Thirdly, there are those from within and without the Christian Homophile movement who affirm not only the permissibility, but the creative joy of homosexual practices based on the belief either that the Bible has been misinterpreted, or that its moral teaching is not decisively relevant to the contemporary situation.

(i) The first category should probably include the evidence submitted to the Wolfenden Committee on behalf of the Church of England's Moral Welfare Council, compiled and edited by D. Sherwin Bailey as Sexual Offenders and Social Punishment.[66] This committee underlined the point that 'inversion' as such is not in itself sinful. Nonetheless the Council recognised that homosexual acts are grave sins though not all equally culpable. They argued, as did Wolfenden, for justice and legal consistency, and concluded that "from the category of immoral sexual acts which are deemed not to be cognizable by the law there would seem to be no justification for excluding male homosexual practices."[67] But this in no way involves the slightest mitigation of the Church's condemnation of moral evil. "It should be clearly understood. . . . that to exempt the private sexual sins of the individual from the scope of the criminal law is not to condone them or dismiss them lightly."[68] Then in 1965, S. B. Babbage's Sex and Sanity appeared, arguing in his chapter on homosexuality for compassion and understanding, but also for 'steadfast reliance on the grace of God'.[69] He quotes an Interim Report produced by a group of Anglican clergy and doctors:

It is a matter of Christian experience that faithful acceptance of a difficult way of life always finds reinforcement in a powerful movement from God towards man.[70]

The revised edition of Anglican theologian H. Waddams 'A New Introduction to Moral Theology (1972) devoted three pages to homosexuality.[71] Waddams distinguishes between those whom he believes are

14

'born with this innate characteristic' and others who 'have resorted to homosexual practices in order to gratify their general sexual desires.' The former, he says, are not morally culpable for their condition, though the latter are; neither can 'physically satisfy their sexual cravings without moral blame'. The Church of England Diocese of Sydney produced a Report on Homosexuality in 1973. It was commended by the Archbishop of Sydney as 'a serious attempt by a responsible committee to come to terms with the problems of homosexuality as it relates to the teaching of the Bible and the welfare of society. It shows clearly', the Archbishop says, 'that growing demand to recognise homosexual conduct as a legitimate life-style constitutes in fact a serious threat to marriage and family life as the fundamental unit of society.' The Report majors on the biblical perspective, criticising Sherwin Bailey's exegesis, and calls on homosexuals to 'cease from practising homosexual acts.' Further, 'while some writers like H. Kimball Jones and N. Pittenger have suggested that Christian churches should accommodate the practising homosexual, the NT evidence points in quite a different direction... From the Church, the homosexual should expect to find understanding and sympathy for human weakness and he should expect to find support and encouragement to live the kind of life which God requires. He will not expect to be blamed or shunned for his homosexual propensity (regardless of its cause), but on the other hand, he will not expect to be received if he does not intend to abide by God's word and stop his homosexual acts, and seek to achieve with God's help such sexual reorientation as may be open to him.[72] In similar vein, the article 'Homosexualism and Homosexuality' in Baker's Dictionary of Christian Ethics (1973) notes that 'those who base their faith on the OT and NT documents cannot doubt that their strong prohibitions of homosexual behaviour make homosexual activity a direct transgression of God's law... While many in our (American) society deny... pathology, and tend to view homosexuality as a form of sexual expression which merely 'differs' from the statistical norm, such attitudes, though appearing humane and altruistic, act to destroy the well-being of the homosexual. They not only discourage his seeking available help, but also encourage him to resign himself to a life which clinical evidence reveals to be increasingly lonely and frustrating.'[73]

The Nationwide Festival of Light published a small pamphlet The Truth in Love in 1975 arguing that Love itself demands the rejection of homosexual practices, which, if accepted, are a mark in society of the judgement of God. David Field wrote, The Homosexual Way - A Christian Option?, in 1976[74] disagreeing with Sherwin Bailey, and concluding that homosexual behaviour must be judged to be wrong on scriptural criteria. 'A loving motive, vastly important though it is, cannot reverse that judgement.' His final chapter considers the Church's role in support, aid and acceptance.

The Nottingham Statements from the National Evangelical Anglican Congress in 1977 urged 'a full welcoming place in the Christian

15

fellowship for the Christian homosexual'. They recognized:

the growing problem of homosexuality and our need for a better
informed understanding of this condition. There should be a
full welcoming place in the Christian fellowship for the Christian
homosexual. Nevertheless we believe homosexual intercourse
to be contrary to God's law and not a true expression of human
sexuality as he has given it. More thought needs to be given to
the pastoral care appropriate to those with this particular need.[75]

This is perhaps the point to note that in December 1977, Third Way
carried an 'Agreed Statement' by three homosexual and three heterosexual evangelicals. They did not reach unanimity in their interpretation of
the Bible, and concluded by saying that 'the practice of homosexuality in
the genital sense will continue to be divisive while our interpretations of
scripture differ.' But they plead for ongoing dialogue rather than the
adoption of entrenched positions on either side. The homosexual has
been 'wrongly feared, ostracised or ignored in most Christian congregations', and his situation needs 'to be considered as much more on a par
with other spiritual and personal problems within the Christian community.'

Two Christian psychiatrists have also written recently on this subject.
In 1975 M. G. Barker wrote a small pamphlet Homosexuality for the
Christian Medical Fellowship, leaning heavily on Thielicke's viewpoint
that homosexuality is a symptom of the Fall by which all men are tainted.
There are thus no grounds for self-righteous discrimination by heterosexuals. Nor are there grounds for idealisation of homosexuality or for
the equation of homosexual with heterosexual. In the Bible, the obligation
to refrain from sexual activity outside marriage is the same whether the
person is homosexual or heterosexual. The Christian Church is called on
to help the homosexual spread his relationships; it should support homosexual equality within the law and society, without accepting that homosexuality is an equally valid sexual experience or supporting the 'right' of
the homosexual to practice if he is a Christian. Then in 1977, the
Paternoster Press issued a small book by psychiatrist Roger Moss:
Christians and Homosexuality. This explores what it means to be homosexual, outlines some medical and psychological considerations, comments
on social prejudice, and seeks to define a Christian viewpoint. Moss discusses the implications of Christian faith for homosexuals, and the
Christian Church's role in relation to homosexuals. He seeks to uphold
the plain warnings of the Old Testament 'harsh though it may seem', and
to recognise the wisdom of doing so. The New Testament confirms the
proscription of homosexual practice, yet prejudice has to be replaced by
a true acceptance, and the real hope in the grace and power of God in his
healing touch can be known.

Three American publications appeared in 1978, all dealing primarily
with the challenges posed to the 'mainline' churches by Christian
homophile movements. From the Presbyterian Church, Jerry Kirk
'speaks out' in The Homosexual Crisis in the Mainline Church[76], arguing

that the prospect of ordaining practising homosexuals will create a 'monumental crisis' in the church. 'Our primary concern must be for a clear understanding of God's truth and how to share that truth with persons in such a way that it liberates and sets free and makes new. We must choose between cheap grace and costly grace. The question we now face is whether we will call one another to be accountable.' Kirk discusses with examples from his own pastoral ministry, the freedom in Christ discovered by those who are brought to repentance for the sin of homosexual practices, while at the same time becoming clearer on the need for repentance himself, and by the Christian church as a whole. Don Williams wrote The Bond That Breaks: Will Homosexuality Split the Church?[77]believing that the demand of homosexual Christians that their lifestyle be sanctioned, and that the calling of some of them to ordination be confirmed, is a crisis which promises to 'disrupt congregations, shatter church structures, throw confusion into time-honoured Biblical interpretation, change the social structure of the country, and revoke our fundamental view of Man as created by God as male and female'. On the other hand, he notes that some see the homosexual challenge as a blessing from God, a view which must not be lightly dismissed. He discusses some contemporary views of homosexuality, expounds the Biblical teaching, and urges a return to a Christian morality based on the revelation of God's Word within which the homosexual person is affirmed as made in the image of God, but homosexual practices are forbidden. At a much more scholarly, and less sensational level, Richard Lovelace has written Homosexuality and the Church[78], again from within the Presbyterian Church. He poses the primary questions for the Church in the context of shifting theological currents in this way:

1. Is the Bible still the supreme guide to Christian faith and practice? What is the role in ethical guidance of reason, experience and the Holy Spirit? How shall we respond to new methods of interpreting the Bible which contradict our previous understanding of its teaching, or which urge us to strike out alone and put aside that teaching?

2. Are all men accepted by God because of the love and grace of Jesus Christ, regardless of their attitudes toward Him and their actions among men? Or must an individual turn to God in a response of repentant faith in Christ, leading to continued growth in holiness, in order to accept the offer of God's forgiveness and enter the sphere of real Christianity?

3. Is situation ethics an adequate guide to the meaning of repentance and the fulfilment of God's will? Should the church's sexual ethic in the late twentieth century endorse all behaviour which seems loving, whether or not it occurs within the traditional limits of gender, marriage and the family?

4. Can the Church tolerate a diversity of convictions and lifestyles in its sexual morality? Or is it responsible to call for some degree of uniformity?[79]

To these questions Lovelace gives a careful historical, biblical and ethical analysis, from which he concludes that there is need for a double repentance: by the homosexual, whom he calls to forego homosexual practices, and draw on the grace and power of the Spirit of Christ for holy living; and by the 'straight' members of the Church, to forego pride, prejudice, hostility and homophobia. For both, the resources of the neglected subject matter of Spiritual Theology (the delivering work of Christ and the sanctifying power of the Spirit) need urgently to be recovered.

(ii) H. Kimball Jones sought to develop a mediating position in Towards a Christian Understanding of the Homosexual in 1966. On the one hand he affirms that 'man is by nature heterosexual in a very fundamental sense, and that his sexual nature can be fulfilled as intended by God only within a relationship of love between a man and a woman.' On the other hand, he regards the Fallen condition of man, and the consequences of the disorder caused by sin to be such that the question has now to be focussed in the form: not 'sex within a heterosexual relationship versus sex within a homosexual relationship', but rather 'sex as a depersonalising force, versus sex as the fulfilment of human relationship'. This distinction allows him to acknowledge that homosexual behaviour in certain circumstances can be morally acceptable, since there is nothing else the person can do.

> The Church must be willing to make the difficult, but necessary
> step of recognising the validity of mature homosexual relationships,
> encouraging the absolute invert to maintain a fidelity to one partner
> when his only other choice would lead to a promiscuous life filled
> with guilt and fear. This would by no means be an endorsement of
> homosexuality by the Church.[80]

A slightly different 'mediating' position is argued for in Charles Curran's Catholic Moral Theology in Dialogue (1972). This included a chapter on the Homophile Movement, in which Curran surveys recent writing. He is favourably inclined towards Thielicke's position, but accepts that in general the homosexual is not responsible for his condition and that celibacy and sublimation are not always possible or even desirable. Therapy, he says, does not offer great promise. 'There are many somewhat stable homosexual unions which afford their partners some human fulfilment and contentment. Obviously such unions are better than homosexual promiscuity.' While attempts should be made, Curran believes, to overcome the condition if possible, at times one may reluctantly accept the compromise that homosexual unions are the only way in which some people can find a satisfying degree of humanity. Curran comments on the 'mistake' of the Gay Lib. Movement, which is the same mistake that the Christian Church has made in the past: namely to identify the person with his homosexuality; one can still love and respect the person, even though one believes his homosexual behaviour falls short of the full meaning of human sexuality.[81]

18

Another Roman Catholic approach can also be mentioned here: The Homosexual Question (1977) by Marc Oriason, a French priest, doctor and psychiatrist. From the basis of wide counselling experience, he seeks to demonstrate how diverse and unique each person's sexuality is. From the viewpoint of Christian faith, sexuality is a field in which the drama of love and tragedy in the Christian life can occur. We are all pilgrims who continually fall short each in his own way of where we want to be, and homosexuality is to be understood in the light of many such lacks in every Christian. 'Clinical experience leads me to believe that a successful homosexual pair involving real love is rare, especially on a long term basis. Rare, but not impossible.'[82]

From an evangelical standpoint, but probably best classed as a 'mediating contribution', Lewis Smedes' Sex for Christians discusses homosexuality under his heading of 'distorted sexuality'. His word to heterosexuals is that they are to assess homosexuality with humility, compassion, and sober moral judgement. His word to homosexuals is that, like every one else, they are called on to be morally responsible in their decision about what to do with their homosexuality. He argues that we must find a way through between two superficial viewpoints: (i) that homosexuality is simply a special form of normal sexuality, different only in that it is a minority condition; and if there is a moral problem it lies with the prejudiced heterosexuals who seek to deprive homosexuals of full equality; and (ii) that homosexuality is a self-chosen perversion, with a desire to distort nature and corrupt others in the process.[83] Smedes affirms that the biblical teaching confirms homosexual practices to be unnatural, 'but I do wish we had a clearer grasp of why homosexuality is unnatural (so is long hair on men: 1 Cor 11.14)'. He suggests that homosexuality contravenes the biblical norms for sexual relationships, which are centred on the 'one flesh' of monogamous heterosexual marriage. Commenting on Karl Barth's strong words on this 'physical, psychological and social sickness, the phenomenon of perversion, decadence and decay', and the need for the 'decisive word of Christian ethics to consist in a warning against entering upon the whole way of life which can only end in the tragedy of concrete homosexuality'[84], Smedes says that this may be ethically sound, but is 'pastorally ineffective'. Smedes rather outlines three steps for responsible confrontation with one's own homosexuality: first, self-knowledge; second, hope - the realisation that change is possible; third, accommodation - which involves considering the call to celibacy, and the need to develop an optimum morality. 'To develop a morality for the homosexual life is not to accept sexual practice as morally commendable. It is, however, to recognise that the optimum moral life within a deplorable situation is preferable to a life of sexual chaos.'[85]

(iii) By contrast with viewpoints which regard homosexual behaviour as either impermissible in all circumstances, or at best only a lesser evil than promiscuity, others have developed a theological position within which homosexual practice can be affirmed. Towards a Quaker View of Sex (1963), for example, pleading that society should recognise

19

homosexuals as human beings, argues that homosexuality is no more blameworthy than left-handedness, and that "it is the nature and quality of a relationship that matters. One must not judge it by its outward appearance, but by its inner worth. Homosexual affection can be as selfless as heterosexual affection, and therefore we cannot see that it is in some way morally worse".[86] Further, they 'see no reason why the physical nature of a sexual act should be the criterion by which the question whether or not it is moral should be decided. An act which (for example) expresses true affection between two individuals and gives pleasure to them both, does not seem to us to be sinful by reason alone of the fact that it is homosexual.'

Canon D. Rhymes and other exponents of 'the New Morality' endorsed the Quaker approach, and in a sermon in Southwark Cathedral on March 10th 1963 observed that 'Much of the prejudice against homosexuality is on the grounds that it is unnatural - unnatural for whom? Certainly not for the homosexual himself.[87]' To this S. B. Babbage responded: 'This kind of reasoning is as misleading as it is mischievous', and quoted with approval Sherwin Bailey's comment in 'The Homosexual and Christian Morals', (They Stand Apart)

> Inversion can no more be regarded as God's will for a person than can, for example, deformity or mental deficiency... The invert is an anomaly whose sexual disorientation bears its own tragic witness to the disordering of humanity by sin... But sympathy with the homosexual's predicament cannot alter the fact that his practices, though congruent with his condition, are objectively unnatural and cannot reasonably be regarded otherwise.[88]

A very important book by the former Professor of Moral Theology at Fordham University, J. J. McNeill, S.J. appeared in 1977. The Church and the Homosexual is a major study from within the Church of Rome, concluding that much of the Church's attitude to homosexuality is 'another example of structured social injustice, equally based on questionable interpretations of Scripture, prejudice and blind adherence to merely human traditions which have been falsely interpreted as the law of nature and of God.' McNeill draws heavily on Sherwin Bailey's 'outstanding scholarly work', largely accepting Bailey's exegesis. His epilogue draws together his conclusions under three headings. First, against the traditional belief that the homosexual condition and homosexual behaviour is contrary to the will of God, McNeill argues that God so created humans that their sexuality is not determined by their biology, and that in the light of today's knowledge (of the Bible and of human sexuality) 'the traditional effort to prove from Scripture and from the natural law that such an orientation is contrary to the will of God no longer has any validity.' Secondly, against the view that the presence of the homosexual in the Christian community is a menace, and threat to family values, and that he should be isolated and 'cured', McNeill believes that homosexuals have an important role to play in the Christian community in preserving and strengthening values such as

interpersonal relations between the sexes, and the development of a
moral understanding of human sexuality outside the procreative context.
And thirdly, against the traditional (Roman Catholic) teaching that
sexual love between homosexuals separates them from the love of God
and places them in danger of eternal damnation, McNeill 'posed the
thesis' that there is the possibility of morally good homosexual
relationships, and that the love which unites the partners can be seen
to unite them more closely to God, and mediate God's presence in our
world.[89]

It is worth noting at this point that also in 1977, and also from within
the Church of Rome, came the Report Human Sexuality, commissioned by
the Catholic Theological Society of America. The authors note that the
trustees of the American Psychiatric Association dropped homosexuality
from the list of recognised mental disorders in 1973. Some of the
Association felt that this was an unscientific concession to the rising
political and social pressures of organised homosexuals, but the action
was upheld in 1974 (6,000 votes for, 4,000 against, 1,000 abstentions).[90]
A recent study of 20,000 'educated higher middle-class subjects' revealed
that more than one third of all males and one fifth of the females had had
homosexual experiences involving orgasm. Public attitude to homosexuality has been extensively researched in the USA. A 1970 study
revealed that 86% of the general American population disapproved of
homosexuality. By 1973, however, the Carnegie Report indicated that
there had been a 'dramatic increase' in young peoples' tolerance of the
homosexual.

A number of other important books have been published specifically
from within the homophile movement. They present a stark contrast to
the 1970 autobiography of Alex Davidson (pseudonymn) The Returns of
Love (I.V.P.) in which the writer struggles with his intellectual
acceptance of the need for chastity, and of the need to see his
homosexual condition as a call from God to celibacy and sublimation.
Thus in Homosexuality from the Inside, (1973), David Blamires sought to
bring Towards a Quaker View of Sex up to date, and illuminate the
difficulties many homosexuals feel 'despite the change of law concerning
male homosexual acts in 1967'. 'My belief is that homosexual relationships have a validity similar to that accorded to heterosexual relationships and that both should be judged by the same moral criteria in so far
a judgement is desirable.[91]

1976 saw the third and revised edition of Norman Pittenger's Time For
Consent (first published with the question mark as Time For Consent? in
the year that the Wolfenden recommendations became law, 1967). The
book was hailed as 'signalling hope and encouragement to many self-
perceived homosexuals, who came to feel that they did not automatically
have to reject Christianity'.[92] It is a plea for Christian openness to the
homosexual, and a plea to the homosexual to believe that there is a place
for him in the Christian fellowship. Pittenger accepts the 'situation
ethic' of a Christian love which is characterised by commitment,

21

mutuality in giving and receiving, genuine tenderness in relationships, intention for faithfulness, hopefulness, and the urgent desire for union with another life or with other lives in as complete and full a sense as is possible for man. If two men or two women are committed together in this sort of love, 'I cannot see, if all this is true, why two persons should be condemned for committing sin, when they desire, as almost invariably they will desire, to act on their love - and that means of course, to engage in physical acts which for them will both express their love and deepen it.[93]'

The Methodist pastor L. Barnett wrote Homosexuality: Time to Tell the Truth in 1975 which popularises for 'young people, their families and friends' the same approach as Pittenger's. N. Pittenger also wrote an essay in the 1977 SCM publication Towards a Theology of Gay Liberation, edited by Malcolm Marcourt. This collection of papers is mostly written from within the homophile movement, some of whose authors are actively involved in the Gay Christian Movement. David Blamires outlines recent literature. There is a section on the Biblical material (R. Norton popularising Bailey, J. Martin challenging Norton, Norton replying that Martin amuses him by his distorting heterosexual bias, and so on). Jim Cotter writes an essay on 'The Gay Challenge to Traditional Notions of Human Sexuality'; N. Pittenger, Giles Hibbert and Michael Keeling offer some theological perspectives on the Gay Lib. debate, and on Homosexual Relationships.

The Gay Christian Movement have a growing list of their own publications, including Sexual Expression and 'Moral Chaos' by Sara Coggin, Freedom and Framework: The shaping of Gay Relationships by Revd. Jim Cotter, Liberation Through Love, by Kennedy Thom, and The Bible and Homosexuality. The latter leans on the conclusions of Sherwin Bailey, quotes McNeill with approval, and develops a position which argues from what it calls 'profoundly biblical insights' that our sexuality is part of our loving, however it is expressed, and that sexuality is good. 'The only difficulty will come if you have a belief that all the scriptures in their every detail are 'india paper', are all equally true. We need to see surely that some truths have been given, and some have been misunderstood, and that the expression of them anyway is limited by language and culture and sheer blindness, and that the Spirit is promised to guide us into the truth.[94]'

In 1978, the Open Church Group published Christian and Gay, a clear statement of an evangelical case for loving homosexual relationships. In the same year, two American evangelicals L. Scanzoni and V. R. Mollenkott wrote Is the Homosexual My Neighbour?, published in UK by SCM Press. This has become a very influential book in American Evangelical circles, and develops the same viewpoint. It exposes the pain and anguish some homosexuals feel, especially Christians who feel an obligation to keep their homosexual inclinations a secret. It asks the Church in the name of Christ, and in the light of his pronouncements on neighbour-love, whether in fact it cares about the suffering and bewilderment which homosexuality can cause. A chapter on the Bible argues that it is silent about the homosexual condition as such, and gives no support to those who base their condemnation of homosexual practices on a mistaken interpretation of it. The sole clear biblical directive relating to the issue, they argue, specifies that Christians are not to judge but to understand; not to condemn relationships out of hand but to assess their quality of commitment. The authors 'invite the entire Christian community to work together to develop a pattern of understanding that expresses Christian principles, and not the prejudices of the world'.[95] A similar case is presented in A Christian Understanding of Human Sexuality, a report (1979) from the Division of Social Responsibility and Faith & Order Committee of the Methodist Church. Space is also made for such a viewpoint in Basil & Rachel Moss Humanity & Sexuality.[96]

Within a context in which social, psychological and theological questions are changing fast, and also in a hypersexualised society like our own in which for increasing numbers of people the only meaning that can be given to the word 'relationship' is a sexual one, it is not surprising that the issue of homosexuality is controversial and emotion-stirring. In particular, homosexual Christians often feel themselves to be pulled in two directions: by the Homophile movement, on the one hand which offers understanding, support, love, care and acceptance; and by their Christian commitment on the other which has often had to be associated with a rejection or a condemnation of what feels to be a centrally important part of their own being. It is therefore very understandable that organisations such as the Gay Christian Movement should be enjoying a growing membership. Understandable - but a strong challenge also to traditional Christian beliefs about and responses to the questions raised by homosexuality. The Statement of Conviction of the GCM reads:

> It is the conviction of the members of the Gay Christian Movement that human sexuality in all its richness is a gift of God gladly to be accepted, enjoyed and honoured as a way of both expressing and growing in love, in accordance with the life and teaching of Jesus Christ: Therefore it is their conviction that it is entirely compatible with the Christian faith not only to love another person of the same sex but also to express that love fully in a personal sexual relationship.

This conviction is translated into the following aims of the Movement:

1. To encourage fellowship, friendship and support among individual gay Christians through prayer, study and action, wherever possible in local groups, and especially to support those gay Christians subjected to discrimination.

2. To help the whole Church re-examine its understanding of human sexuality and to work for a positive acceptance of gay relationships

23

within the framework outlined in the Statement of Conviction, so that all homosexuals may be able to live without fear of rejection or recrimination, and that homosexual Christians may be able to contribute fully to the life and ministry of the Church.

3. To encourage members to witness to their Christian faith and experience within the gay community, and to witness to their convictions about human sexuality within the Church.

4. To maintain and strengthen links with other gay Christian groups both in Britain and elsewhere.

Specifically the GCM affirms that homosexuality is unusual, but natural; and that a homosexual person is one who finds fulfilment in a love which involves another of the same sex. ('Of course you may think that the purpose of sex is just to produce children. But surely it can also give a richness and depth to relationships of love and in turn create yet more love?'). The GCM firmly believes that it 'is not selling out on Christian truth. It is working for the very love and freedom that Christ brings to his people.'

The existence of this and other Christian Homophile movements does throw out a challenge to Christians who think in terms of the traditional Christian approach to the question of homosexuality. The challenge appears to be a fourfold one: Is homosexuality an abnormal condition or is it a 'natural' orientation, part of God's good creation? What are Christian norms for sexual behaviour, and how should homosexual practices be viewed within these norms? Has the Bible been misunderstood in the traditional interpretation which condemns all sexual behaviour between members of the same sex? What place do homosexuals have in the Christian fellowship, or is the creation of 'fear of rejection and recrimination' the only appropriate Christian response? This fourfold challenge probes to the heart of the whole meaning of and Christian understanding of human sexual identity. It will form the basis for our discussion in Part 2.

NOTES

[1] E. M. Forster, Maurice, Penguin Books 1977 edition, p. 9.

[2] Ibid p. 221.

[3] Report of the Committee on Homosexual Offences and Prostitution (1957).

[4] H. Ruitenbeek, Homosexuality, a Changing Picture, Souvenir Press, (1973) p. 72.

[5] H. Ruitenbeek, Homosexuality: a Changing Picture (1973), p. 13. cf. also the research of M. Schofield Sociological Aspects of Homosexuality (Longmans, 1965).

[6] op. cit., p. 13.

[7] Ibid.

[8] D. J. West, Homosexuality Re-examined, (Duckworth, 1977), p. 246.

[9] Ibid.

[10] Referred to in J. Kleinig, 'Reflections on Homosexuality', Australian Journal of Christian Education, Papers 59, Sept. 1977.

[11] G. Hocquenghem Homosexual Desire (Allison and Busby, ET 1978)

[12] Ibid. p. 9.

[13] From the tape recording of the meeting.

[14] A. C. Kinsey et. al., Sexual Behaviour in the Human Male (W. B. Saunders 1948) Sexual Behaviour in the Human Female (W. B. Saunders 1953).

[15] Kinsey op. cit., (1948), p. 638.

[16] Ibid. p. 651.

[17] W. Lindford Rees A Short Textbook of Psychiatry (Hodder & Stoughton Unibooks, 1976²), p. 231.

[18] E. Glover, The Problem of Homosexuality, Institute for the Study and Treatment of Delinquency, (1954), p. 6.

[19] cf. C. W. Socarides, The Overt Homosexual (Grune and Stratton, 1968) and refs. cited; cf. also chapter 2 of this Latimer Study, and refs. cited, etc.

[20] cf. ref. 19.

[21] Homosexuality and Prostitution a memorandum of evidence prepared by a special committee of the Council of the British Medical Association (BMA, London 1955), p. 49.

[22] Op. cit., p. 30.

[23] Op. cit., p. 92.

[24] A. Ellis, Reason and Emotion in Psychotherapy (Lyle Stuart, N. J. 1962), p. 241f.

[25] Op. cit., p. 242.

[26] Op. cit., p. 246.

[27] Op. cit., p. 252.

[28] Ibid.

[29] Irving Bieber et. al., Homosexuality: a Psychoanalytic Study (Basic Books, 1962).

[30] Ibid. p. 303.

[31] Ibid. p. 304.

[32] Ibid.

[33] Ibid. p. 319.

[34] I. Bieber 'A Discussion of "Homosexuality: The Ethical Challenge",' Journal of Consulting and Clinical Psychology 44 No 2, (1976) p. 163ff.

[35] Antony Storr, Sexual Deviation (Penguin, 1964), 70f, 81f. He says that 'there is a great deal to suggest that the male homosexual is made, not born, and that his sexual preference in adult life is determined by the emotional influences to which he has been exposed in early childhood' (p. 91) 'Research into family background...has already yielded results which show that certain specific patterns are particularly likely to produce a male homosexual son.' (p. 83) He also says: 'The average man who has a wife to go home to has little idea of the depths of lonliness to which homosexuals can sink, or of the strength of the compulsive urge for sexual contact which drives them... Public opinion is gradually changing towards a more liberal attitude (than the law which in 1964 condemned homosexual behaviour as criminal)... But the homosexual way of life is intrinsically unsatisfying, and we should make every effort to

encourage research which will teach us ways of preventing the homosexual pattern from becoming established and of altering it wherever possible.' (p. 90).

[36] cf. H. Merskey and W. L. Tonge Psychiatric Illness (Balliere, Tindall & Cassell, 1965) included homosexuality within a discussion of 'Sexual Perversion' (p. 193), commenting that as regards treatment and prognosis, much depends on whether the patient is still in the toils of a delayed adolescence... or is a true invert.' (p. 195).

[37] cf. W. Linford Rees, A Short Textbook of Psychiatry (Hodder and Stoughton Unibooks, 1976)

[38] Ruitenbeek, op. cit., p. 79.

[39] Op. cit., p. 99.

[40] From promotional leaflet of Gay Christian Movement.

[41] cf. Bieber, JCCP, 44, (1976), 163ff. cf. also J. R. Snortum et. al., Psychological Reports 24, (1969), 763ff.

[42] C. W. Socarides, The Overt Homosexual (Grune and Stratton, 1968).

[43] Ibid. p. 5

[44] Ibid. p. 6

[45] Ibid. p. 7

[46] cf. e. g. G. C. Davison 'Homosexuality: The Ethical Challenge', Journal of Consulting and Clinical Psychology, 44, (1976), 157ff.; the paper to which Bieber (1976) is a reply.

[47] H. Ruitenbeek, Homosexuality: a Changing Picture (1973), p. 13.

[48] J. Babuscio We Speak For Ourselves (SPCK 1976) describing G. Weinberg Society and the Healthy Homosexual (Doubleday, 1973).

[49] Antony Grey, Counselling News 19, February 1978.

[50] Ruitenbeek, op. cit.

[51] Daily Telegraph April 18th 1979. The researchers are best known for their books: W. H. Masters and V. E. Johnson, Human Sexual Response (J. A. Churchill, 1966), and Human Sexual Inadequacy (J. A. Churchill, 1970).

[52] For refs. 52-55 cf. D. Sherwin Bailey, Homosexuality and the Western Christian Tradition, 82ff. Tertullian On Modesty, chap. 4; The Writings of Quintus Sept. Flor. Tertullianus,Vol 3. Ante-Nicene Christian Library, (Edinburgh, 1870) p. 64.

[53] Saint Chrysostom, A select library of Nicene and Post-Nicene Fathers of the Christian Church, ed. P. Schaff, Vol 11, Eerdmans (1969), p. 355, Homily on Rom 1. 26-7.

[54] Saint Augustine, Confessions (Penguin edition 1961); p. 65; Book III/8 referring to 'sins against nature... like the sin of Sodom.'

[55] The Summa Theologica of St. Thomas Aquinas (trans.; Burnes Oates and Washbourne Ltd. 1921); Q 154, article 12 'Of the Parts of Lust', p. 160. 'In sins contrary to nature, whereby the very order of nature is violated, an injury is done to God, the Author of nature... Among sins against nature... the most grievous is the sin of bestiality, because use of the due species is not observed... After this comes the sin of sodomy, because use of the right sex is not observed...

[56] cf. Richard F. Lovelace, Homosexuality and the Church (Fleming H. Revell, N. J.; (1978), p. 19, referring to Luther's Lectures on Romans on Rom 1. 24f.

[57] J. Calvin, Commentary on Romans, (Oliver and Boyd, 1960 edn.) on Rom 1.26; cf. also Commentary on First Corinthians (on 6.9-11).

[58] H. Thielicke, The Ethics of Sex (James Clarke, ET 1964), 269ff.

[59] Ibid p. 282.

[60] Ibid p. 283.

[61] Ibid p. 287.

[62] D. Sherwin Bailey Homosexuality and the Western Christian Tradition, Longmans (1955).

[63] David Blamires in Towards a Theology of Gay Liberation (SCM, 1977) p. 9.

[64] Sherwin Bailey, op.cit., p. 157.

[65] Ibid.

[66] D. Sherwin Bailey ed. Sexual Offenders & Social Punishment published for the Church of England Moral Welfare Council by the Church Information Board (1956).

[67] Ibid. p. 87: "The Criminal Aspects of Homosexual Sin".

[68] Ibid.

[69] S. B. Babbage, Sex and Sanity, (Hodder and Stoughton, 1965), p. 75.

[70] The Problem of Homosexuality (Church Information Board, p. 15).

[71] Herbert Waddams, A New Introduction to Moral Theology, (SCM revised edition 1972), 145f.

[72] 'Report on Homosexuality' Report of the Ethics and Social Questions Committee to the Synod of the Church of England Diocese of Sydney, 1973.

[73] Armand M. Nicholi II, 'Homosexualism and Homosexuality' in Carl F. H. Henry, ed. Baker's Dictionary of Christian Ethics (Eerdmans 1973), p. 295.

[74] David Field The Homosexual Way - a Christian Option? (Bramcote, Grove Books, 1976). A slightly expanded version with a pastoral chapter is now being published in USA.

[75] The Nottingham Statement, Falcon Books 1977 section R3.

[76] Jerry Kirk, The Homosexual Crisis in the Mainline Church (Thomas Nelson, N.Y., 1978).

[77] Don Williams, The Bond That Breaks: Will Homosexuality Split the Church? (BIM Inc. Los Angeles, 1978).

[78] Richard F. Lovelace Homosexuality and the Church, (Fleming H. Revell Co., Old Tappan, N.J., 1978).

[79] Ibid. p. 11f.

[80] H. Kimball Jones, Towards a Christian Understanding of the Homosexual, (Association Press, N.Y., 1966), p. 108.

[81] Charles E. Curran, Catholic Moral Theology in Dialogue, (1972, Notre Dames Press edition 1976), p. 219.

[82] Marc Oriason The Homosexual Question, (Search Press 1977), p. 120.

[83] Lewis B. Smedes, Sex For Christians (Eerdmans, 1976) p. 62ff.

[84] Referring to K. Barth, Church Dogmatics III/4 (James Clarke, ET 1961), p. 166.

[85] Smedes, op.cit., p. 73.

[86] A. Heron ed. Towards a Quaker View of Sex (Friends Home Service Committee, 1963); 21f.

[87] Quoted in S. B. Babbage, op.cit., p. 74.

[88] Ibid.

27

[89] J. J. McNeill, S. J. The Church and the Homosexual (Darton Longman and Todd, 1977).

[90] A. Kosnik et. al., Human Sexuality, New Directions in Catholic Thought (Search Press, 1977) 186ff.

[91] David Blamires, essay in Towards a Theology of Gay Liberation, p. 21f.

[92] Ibid. p. 18.

[93] Norman Pittenger Time For Consent (SCM revised edition 1976), p. 75.

[94] Gay Christian Movement pamphlet, The Bible and Homosexuality p. 17.

[95] Letha Scanzoni and Virginia Ramey Mollenkott, Is the Homosexual My Neighbour? Another Christian View (SCM 1978), quotation from back cover.

[96] Basil & Rachel Moss Humanity and Sexuality, (C10 1978), esp. para. 67

Since this chapter was written, a number of books and articles have been published, of especial significance the Anglican Report Homosexual Relationships: a contribution to discussion (1979), and Peter Coleman's Christian Attitudes to Homosexuality (1980), together with many study guides and comments on the Anglican and Methodist Reports. The autumn 1979 issue of Christian Action, including articles by Monica Furlong, Helen Oppenheimer, Rowan Williams, Jack Dominian and Jim Cotter, was given to comment on the Reports. Michael Green, David Holloway and David Watson responded to the Anglican Report in The Church and Homosexuality (1980), and recent issues of Theology and of Crucible (the Journal of the Church of England Board for Social Responsibility) have carried articles on the subject.

The two first named books require particular comment.

The Anglican Report carries the conclusions of a Working Party, together with a critical assessment of the Working Party's conclusions by members of the Board for Social Responsibility. The Working Party offered chapters on the social setting of homosexuality, and on medical and biblical evidence; it gave a theological and ethical analysis, and commented on the legal, social and pastoral issues raised. The recommendation which has provoked most controversy is the Working Party's judgement that 'there are circumstances in which individuals may justifiably choose to enter into a homosexual relationship with the hope of enjoying a companionship and physical expression of sexual love similar to that which is found in marriage.' To this the Board for Social Responsibility responded that the burden of proof would lie very heavily on anyone who wished to counter specific and unqualified biblical condemnation of practices by appealing to unspecified 'ethical teachings' of Jesus, and criticism has been made of the Report's methodology as well as its exegesis and conclusions.

Peter Coleman's book is almost certain to become the standard resource on this subject. It is scholarly and sensitive, summarizing material from a wide range of sources. His initial chapter tentatively concludes that while causes remain obscure, and though sexual preference is non-voluntary, moral responsiblity remains for each person's chosen lifestyle. A very full exploration of the biblical and extra-biblical texts is given, and Coleman comments: 'Whatever status is granted to them by contemporary Christians, the texts sufficiently show that the biblical writers condemned homosexual practices.' The survey of attitudes from the early church to the Wolfenden recommendations includes reference to such 'famous victims' as Wilde, Vaughan, Headlam, and Casement, and to the 'rescue work' of the White Cross League. The role of Churchmen in the processes of law reform is fully documented, and the increasing flood of contemporary literature is then surveyed, concluding with the report of the Anglican Working Party referred to above.

2. OF HOMOSEXUALITY: THE CURRENT STATE OF KNOWLEDGE

by A. W. STEINBECK*, University of New South Wales, Australia.

"None of us lives to himself
and none of us dies to himself"   Paul, Saul of Tarsus

Foreword and Definition

THE homosexual as such does not exist, but persons who at times fantasize, feel and act homosexually do. Their random thoughts may drift towards homosexual interests just as the random thoughts of others turn to their basic interests. Many other people at some point in their lives have homosexual fantasies and impulses, which may or may not lead to homosexual behaviour. Homosexual desire can vary from an ephemeral erotic arousal cued by another of the same sex to an unthinking, unceasing and sometimes frantic pursuit of homoerotic contacts carried to the point of orgasm. Any definition should probably stipulate that for a response to be properly homosexual, there must be active or passive sexual arousal by another of the same sex at some level of consciousness, be it in dream, fantasy, impulse or act. To call a person a homosexual usually implies a commitment to a homosexual life-style and/or identification with a homosexual sub-culture.

No definition will satisfy all the data, and a subjective element is always present; the emphasis and sophistication of the definition varies with the experience, the personality and the emphasis of the user.[1] Even if we start from the linguistic agreement that homo(s) refers to same-sex relationships whereas hetero(s) implies relationships between the sexes, it is still possible that the perception of particular acts by those within a homosocial grouping may differ from the interpretations placed on them by society at large, and equally, that the acts may not necessarily portend true homosexuality. Vernacular descriptions are usually unfortunate and often erroneously imply sexual inversion or third sex interpretations. Karyotype descriptions are mostly irrelevant.[2] The homosexuality of some relationships may be dismissed by clinicians on technical grounds, or misinterpreted by homosexuals themselves.

Questions for the Christian Believer

The Christian faith presupposes that God has revealed his purposes, particularly in relation to human behaviour. An absolute standard of how human beings should behave is allied to a high view of the destiny of persons in relation to God. The Christian in society is therefore called upon to maintain God's standards while standing, in compassion, alongside those who like himself, have in certain respects fallen beneath this destiny. The Christian clinician, unlike the humanist who denies an eternal point of reference, knows that sometimes he must console but not condone. For example, he accepts that it is the faculty that provides the facility, and the facility is determined by the faculty, whereas the humanist, not accepting this principle as part of the objectively real world, may be prepared simply to allow the individual to follow his own reason or desire.

Christian believer and clinician, while standing firm in belief, must be able to acknowledge that other views exist, and to understand them sympathetically. One should always be alert to the possibility, as was mentioned earlier, of misinterpreting what one sees in the behaviour of others who interpret the world differently from us.

Cultural Factors
The Christian is not excused from learning what scientific studies have revealed about homosexuality. Thus the publication of Sexual Behaviour in the Human Male made many aware for the first time of biological norms different from their own. Some young males became perturbed or affronted because the norms described in the report made them appear inadequate. Later studies suggested that application of the label "homosexual" to, for instance, situations where males played female roles, might be less accurate than citing them as cases of inversion. Another possible approach to determining whether homosexuality or heterosexuality was involved was by ascertaining the genetic sexes of the persons involved.[3] Other investigators discounted homosexuality in those relationships where mutual masturbation did not include oral or anal behaviour, or where certain psychic responses were absent. In relationships involving anal behaviour, it was argued by some that the active male could be regarded as behaving heterosexually whereas only the passive male's behaviour was homosexual.[4] Such disputes over nomenclature run the risk of diverting our attention from the significance of homosexual behaviour.

Further confusions arise when the homosexual seems, as many do, to be better informed of the literature on homosexual culture than the clinician. Some homosexual persons deny the ascription of "real homosexuality" to others who might ordinarily be so judged, because they expect a certain level of conscious fantasy, impulse or action. Thus it is pointed out that in tribal groups where an adult male and young boy become partners according to custom, "homosexuality" takes on a meaning different from that which it has in a culture strongly influenced by Christian values. Similarly, members of a Christianized culture may vary in the guilt they feel at having ephemeral fantasies or impulses of a homosexual kind. That some have such fantasies and impulses against their wishes is evident from anamneses. With some reservations one can say that the Kinsey ratings of 0 to 6, where 0 is the opposite of the exclusively homosexual rating of 6, are also open to such criticisms. The fact of a younger person wishing, for example, to identify with an older person of the same sex, because of the admired virtues and attributes of the older is not in itself indicative of homosexuality, though some would say that this depends on the intensity of the desire. Certainly it seems necessary to distinguish clearly between impulse as such, and impulse carried through to fantasy or act.

The central semantic problem is the defining of normality, as opposed to abnormality or deviant behaviour. Traditionally, adult homosexual behaviour has been dealt with as individual psychopathology.[5] This presupposes a diagnosis of "disease"; acceptable perhaps in the case of the individual who desires to be heterosexual and is in conflict, but unacceptable to those who find personal satisfaction and peace in a homosexual life-style or sub-culture. The first may present themselves to a clinician because they see their depression, aggression, personal inadequacy or sadism creating internal or external conflict. For them, treatment may afford relief and modify behaviour, while leaving the basic homosexual disposition unaltered.

It is insufficient to know that a person is a homosexual without knowing the kind of person he is in other respects. Some homosexuals colour their histories with explanatory theories of their own; others, fearing legal or social constraints or suspecting that the observer is unsympathetic, obscure pertinent facts; and there are some who, sensing that the clinician is ill at ease, exaggerate with intent to horrify him.

Likewise the personality of the observer must be taken into account. Tenacious theories can bias even statistical correlations, and no personality profile can be set up without a theoretical base.

Great variety must also be recognized in the degree of overt expression by the individual of homosexual tendencies. Some immerse themselves in the homosexual sub-culture, others eschew it and prefer the ordinary world, others live in both. Some live almost in two different worlds, either by isolating their homosexual contacts from their wider social life (whereas others don't) or have a work world where their patterns of life conform but a non-work world of homosexual activity, life and living. Some cultured persons studiously avoid gay meeting places, or are unaware of them, and regard gay queens and their life style as out of place; except that they themselves may at times cross-dress, enjoy party life, charades, physical contact and group feeling for homosexual reasons.

Some homosexuals have a life so hidden that neither clinician nor closest friend suspects its existence. They are understandably uncertain how others will react, and fear that reactions will be based only on knowledge of the popular and cruder sort. Many have never gone to a "market place" or "cruising area" for their personality is not of the "market" and is affronted by such behaviour. Some give expression to their desires only by voyeurism in public lavatories. Some fight their homosexuality; others glory in it, and many accept it as a natural way of life.

It is not clear from research whether people of homosexual disposition tend towards certain kinds of occupation in preference to others. There is some overseas evidence of this being so.[6] The research worker must beware of basing his findings on too small a sample; say, the university

31

students or religious and professional persons of one sex whom he may meet clinically. He needs to know something also of the leather-jacketed dwellers in domitory suburbs unlike his own; to understand the import, in some cultures, of such personal labels as "butch", "dyke", "hustler", "closet queen", "piss elegant", "Curzon Street cowboy", etc.; and to obtain some notion of the undisclosed number who behaved homosexually in adolescence and early adult life but do so no longer. Many, it seems, have resolved their conflicts over sex and gender identity and entered into successful marriage, a potentially bisexual or a bisexual relationship.

There is a group who with strident fervour have elected to identify themselves to the media as a vocal and persecuted minority. Often they attack church groups - understandably, because they feel threatened by the churches' stance, while conversely the churches are apprehensive of their evangelistic zeal.

A different range of problems arises with people who find their cultural sexual identity threatened by transient fantasies, or by the apparent rejection of their masculinity or feminity,[7] or by the discovery that marriage has not subdued their homosexual impulses.[8]

Finally, there is a class of acts, possibly arising from internal homosexual conflict, which are bizarre or "sick" and sometimes brutal.[9] Brutality within the culture is restricted but can be ritualistic; it can also represent punishment meted out for various reasons.

Human Sexuality: Body Features
The problem of sexuality, of the male and the female in their maleness and femaleness, has been confused by over-emphasis on particular cultural connotations of masculinity (or virility - which to some is an extension of masculinity) and femininity, and the counter-attacks of radical psychologists.

An individual's sex is potentially defined or determined by the zygotic sex resulting from fertilization of the ovum. This is called the karyotype (46, XX is female; 46, XY is male). If it is normal, then the gametes and initial divisions of the fertilized ovum are normal, otherwise chromosomal abnormalities, both sex and autosomal, could occur. This zygotic sex has been termed by some, notably moralists, the "given sex". It can only be potential until brought to full development by a sequence of carefully regulated processes. The primitive gonad must appear and differentiate. The Y-chromosome is associated with development of the testis which confers maleness upon the potentially ambisexual foetal body.[10] The ovary, or abnormally a dysgenetic ovary, allows foetal development to proceed in a female manner. Thus, gonadal sex is established. With differentiation of the foetal gonad, the duct system will normally conform: in the female, the Müllerian system proceeds toward uterus and fallopian tubes and the labioscrotal folds, and in the absence of androgen, leads to labia enclosing the vaginal

32

sinus; in the male, the Müllerian system is suppressed and the Wolffian system under influence of androgen develops into spermatic ducts, etc., labioscrotal folds fusing to produce a scrotum enclosing the testes. The phallus is stimulated to develop into a penis: with subsidiary structures this organ encloses the urethra whereas the phallus remains separate from the urethra in the female to become the clitoris.[11] This is the situation at birth when the nursery and legal sex is nominated, unless there is any doubt. If there is, then at the least karyotype and other appearances need review. These nursery appearances determine the sex of rearing and the basis of education for the psychological sex, gender role and cultural behaviour for that sex.[12]

Approaching the age of puberty, although psychologically sexual behaviour may precede physical change through cultivation,[13] the hypothalamic-pituitary endocrine complex is activated through an inbuilt mechanism or "biological clock". Releasing hormones proceed in increasing quantity from the hypothalamic area to the pituitary gland which releases increasing quantities of trophic hormones. These stimulate the appropriate end-organs and glands, including the gonads, to produce their hormones and subsequently those physical changes which are characteristic of the pubertal process. Thus, secondary sexual characteristics become evident, the body assumes features of an adult male or female (maleness and femaleness) and the appearances thus confirm, or in the case of abnormalities variously deny, the sex of rearing.[14]

In homogeneous development from zygote onwards, the physical characteristics of the individual will be appropriate for the given sex, the characteristics otherwise being those for the genetic background to which the individual is heir and which may lead to secondary sexual features (such as lack of beard or small breasts from Chinese forebears) which may not be culturally and socially acceptable. In this regard, the appearance of pubertal gynaecomastia is physiologically normal; but if it is excessive and a female breast is suggested, it may be disconcerting to adolescents and need surgical correction. The development of some hirsutism is normal for a female but, culturally and socially, glabrous skin is preferred. Thus, what is iso-sexual and not heterosexual can produce conflicts that the individual may never resolve. Today, even normal sexual or pubic hair in women may prove unacceptable because of clothing fashions, whether at the beach or elsewhere. The axillae (in the armpits) have long since succumbed. Actual (or even implied but virtual) heterosexual features, especially in females, imply an abnormal puberty; failure of menarche (established primary amenorrhoea) also suggests abnormality. Regular rhythmic menstruation implies normal female hormone sequences. Absence of breast development and failure of menstruation imply basic disturbances. Penile development at puberty implies androgen production and, in general, testicular enlargement confirms seminiferous tubule development. The female is fully mature physically when ovulatory menstrual cycles appear and the male when semen containing normal amounts of spermatozoa is produced. Both are then potentially fertile and the male should be capable of insemination.

Around this epoch secondary personality changes occur, associated with female and male pudor and the heightened awareness of the sexual body and gender roles. Whereas an ego-identity (I - the person) was being established before, a sex-identity (I - the person with a sexual identity) becomes the concern of most individuals. This may only be described by a knowledge of the day-dreaming, erotic fantasies and dreams, play activity and general behaviour trends in conformity with the customs and attitudes of cultural groups and larger subgroups.[15] At this time, a normally healthy, loving and caring family environment is essential. Abnormal male-female relationships in the family may cause conflict for family dependants. A supportive and "drawing out" role is as essential for the family as is the maintenance of normal relationships within, by and outside the family. The body image of the individual cannot be forgotten in this context nor how the individual sees himself overall.

Human Sexuality: Hormone Features
The influences of hormones upon cerebral and personality development are descriptively obvious. The male who lacks testes, or whose testes fail to secrete adequate testosterone, may never become a normal male if hormone is only given at the time puberty would already have taken place in his peers. The later this replacement takes place, the more evident may be the failure, and replacement should precede the age at which puberty would be expected, for hormonal changes precede physical effect. Whether antenatal hormonal influences are relevant in man is uncertain, but testosterone given to pregnant rhesus monkeys can influence the behaviour of the androgenized female offspring; it also induces abnormality of pituitary-ovarian function.[16] These monkeys behave instinctively but man has the ability to behave in terms of a human mind-brain relationship or from social experience.

It may be that hormonal influences in foetal life influence the effectiveness of social experience[17] and this is suggestive in some instances of abnormal hormone production in the female foetus. However, the situation as reported is not strictly comparable with the normal. In a pack of dogs, dogs will follow another male with an oestrogen secreting testicular tumour and attempt to couple as with a bitch; they respond instinctively to hormonal influences and do not recognize the nature of the dog sought. The mounting activity practised by young animals is independent of gonadal hormone production in some. Likewise, sexual and play behaviour can be influenced by rearing conditions in rhesus monkeys,[18] a fact which is sometimes neglected. In the male foetus, testosterone production can start at week 8-10 after conception. Plasma levels at 20 weeks may approach fully adult values (at the time of differentiation of the genitalia and possibly of the hypothalamus), only to decline toward parturition. The female foetus has no such capability and so would seem at greater risk if androgen were produced. (See above.) The spontaneous experiment occurs in the quantitative enzymatic abnormality of adrenal dyshormono-genesis (congenital adrenogenital syndrome) and affected girls may well have fewer apparent female interests than expected. This appears to have been the case in some large sibships where the syndrome occurred, and where comparison is valid. However, there is a wide diversity within the syndrome and, significantly, evidence suggests that in rats the oestrogen (female hormone) is the active agent at the brain level, in which case androgen would be its precursor.

Hormone parameters are measurable in blood and tissue and their patterns can be studied by sensitive and accurate methods. In absolute hormone deficiency, physical effects are known, and psychological concomitants can be described. This is applicable to both androgen and oestrogen deficiency states. The female with an excessive production of androgens (or undue androgen sensitivity) before puberty, and provided her femaleness is established experientially, is more likely to suffer emotionally than to react physically, although this may happen. It is reassuring to observe girls, who may have reacted ambivalently because of clitoral enlargement[19] or voice and body characteristics nevertheless establishing femaleness though continuing to suffer emotionally because of their other female, or male-like, characteristics. Some indeed have sought to establish femaleness by aggressive femininity and some have been original female liberationists; some have had intense sexual urges with much personal conflict, others have acted them out; and some without such urges have sought to establish their femaleness by aggressive promiscuity or unreal coquetry. Some have established a homosexual relationship, not always with persons with ambiguous genitalia. Equally, lack of secondary sexual characteristics can result in florid promiscuity.[20] Conversely, many avoid heterosexual contact although some marry without complaint or query. Psychological puberty may indeed antedate physical puberty if the educational climate is so weighted and established; pre-pubertal girls may react to boys in an adolescent pattern taught them by the media and their mothers. Grossly hypogonodal boys may attempt intercourse to establish manhood, and often with someone much younger.

Deficiency of androgen, short stature and known aspermia led in one case to defloration urges and aberrant sexual behaviour in a 46, XX male. He needed to compensate for nature's error by acting out his gender role like his sex peers, always without fulfilment because of infertility. Micro-penis abnormality appeared to disturb him and make for aggression. Two other 46, XX males (and they are unusual) were also potent to their satisfaction but might have been impotent if their abnormality (karyotype and aspermia) had been over-emphasized or the existential significance of a 46, XX karyotype grasped. The same has applied to some 47, XXY males in whom potency was totally normal but poorly established or lacking from an androgen deficiency. Like an otherwise normal male, if their sexuality was affronted, as for example by the confirmation of infertility, then their potency could be destroyed. Impotence or inability to find physical satisfaction in sexual intercourse may occur even when

35

all hormonal and neurological parameters are entirely normal, thus confirming its psychological dependence in these instances.

As an extension of this problem, psychological hypogonadism, whether established behaviourally or resulting from existential depression, may occur in adolescents and young adults notwithstanding a normal phenotype that should have a concomitant normal body image. Sometimes the father has suppressed sexuality development, whereas at others the mother is guilty. None the less, the picture of a male university student checking his sexual progress by referring to the Kinsey report and being stricken with his inadequacy or confused by his scores is a poignant social comment; the more so when his girlfriend was asked to check his report. The comment of a call-girl upon a university medical student testing his sexual prowess was no less poignant but equally disastrous for his well-being.

Puberty in the Homosexual
Obviously, puberty in the homosexual can only be studied retrospectively. The evidence suggests that, if the pattern for homosexuality is established in the early development years, then the hormones at puberty bring it to full expression. Once established the pattern seems resilient. However, there seems to be no way to predict which anatomically normal boy or girl will become erotically homosexual. Equally, notwithstanding full biographical details and psychological theory to the contrary, it is not possible to predict which anatomically normal boy or girl will become erotically heterosexual or bisexual. The pubertal hormones appear to establish the sexual urges for all according to their disposition.

Genital Sex and Homosexuality
In homosexual persons, there have been no problems or confusion over genital sex, except in several instances of ambiguous genitalia or ambiguous secondary sexual development. This appears to be usual in homosexual life and the homosexual accepts his genitalia as they are, seldom hating or hiding them.

This is in contradistinction to those suffering from the gender dysphoria state of transsexualism or transsexuality where the penis of the male is hated,frequently not looked upon and mostly retroflexed between the thighs.[2] Developmental studies have given little support to the suggestions that homosexuality is a developmental condition, due to an hormonal abnormality, which precludes full expression of heterosexuality. It is impossible on the evidence from endocrinology to claim that homosexuality is of a developmental nature, which might obviate responsibility for behaviour patterns. In view of the attitudes of 47,XYY individuals with a normal general intelligence it would be doubtful that responsibility would be negated. Equally there is no substance to the claim that, as animals demonstrate sexual play with individuals of the same sex, homosexuality is an inherent and natural condition. Indeed, serious observers have not claimed this. Allowing that it is natural for animals so to act as a preparation for sexual maturity and mating, and as a rehearsal function in preparation for the instinctive reproductive behaviour of the adult animals, whether seasonal or not, there is no homology with man. The dominance in the human of the mind-brain over the body and its potential control of instinctive reactions suggests a basis for the control of unwanted erotic impulses and urges to act in hetero-sexual situations. Obviously pathology may arise. Similar considerations apply for homosexual impulses.

To argue homology from animal behaviour is to render man less than man, with less than human personality. Penile erection during aggression or its equivalent is noted at times in man, and can occur with equivalent responses, including bruxism, in man during REM sleep correlated with dreaming.[22] This suggests a neurally related response subserved by older portions of the brain. Penile erection occurs in stimulated adolescents, often to their dismay, in pleasant heterosexual circumstances. Adult man learns to control these and similar reactions because of his cerebral dominance, and mostly will not react instinctively, as for example a monkey might.[23]

It is significant that a number of female homosexuals, some in confirmed relationships, seek pregnancy by means of artificial insemination. By contrast there are others who seek hysterectomy to rid themselves of menstrual problems and their femininity. Women "married" to female-to-male transsexuals have craved motherhood and been supported in this by their "husband", although initially they had accepted the impossibility of parenthood, sic motherhood. At times, some female homosexuals appear conscious of their deprivation and intercourse becomes less than satisfactory for them. Presumably, there is absent or inadequate vaginal sensation although the psychosexual factors remain strong and the love of the partner is very evident. An erotic response can probably never correspond to the authentic,[24] notwithstanding the claims of radical psychology.[25]

If committed homosexuality be regarded as symptomatic of defective personality organization, sources of inadequacy in relation to one's peers of the same genital sex may appear significant both in causation and subsequent anxiety. Most males have never fought their peers. There may be a feeling of inadequacy as a sexual performer as part of a general feeling of inadequacy before homosexual desire arises. Later, the person eventually succumbs to these desires often after efforts of suppression. It is possible to develop a devastating self concept in this situation that others similarly affected may emphasize and strengthen. Experiences of certain types, or occurring in the context of certain biographical details, appear common, such as disturbed relationships with parents, and parental discord that destroys concepts of normal male-female relationships. The absent father, dominant mother or father-destroying mother are commonly found. At times a well-loved homosexual relative introduces the person to the culture. The relative may have earned his position. Some psychoanalysts regard homosexuality as a quantitative matter, others as basically a qualitative matter. The appearance of homosexuality in a prepsychotic personality may represent decompensation of the personality and it does occur in schizophrenia. However, these incidences bear no relationship to the usual instance of the homosexual disposition. In general, the appearance of homosexuality in a psychosis can be equated with decompensation, disorganization or lack of inhibition in the personality.

This argument is applied to alcohol or drug induced homosexual behaviour. Deprivation and/or lack of personality strength are the factors suggested for homosexuality among prisoners, sailors and indentured labourers where the sexual urge in a homosocial group may become paramount. Delinquent behaviour is probably in a different category, likewise dormitory activity in a boarding school or similar establishment. Some activity can be pure affectation or done for group acceptance.

Causative Factors
Several empirical facts and factors can be emphasized in discussing the causation of homosexuality. There is no genetic or chromosomal aberration underlying the disposition of homosexuality. Among commited and transitional homosexuals, transvestites and transsexuals, the defined chromosomal abnormalities have been 47, XXY (or variants e. g., 46, XY/47, XXY) or 47, XYY (normal or mildly hypogonadal phenotype) with no abnormalities among females. Thus, there is no constant chromosomal association with the condition. Although fears are expressed by some parents that their anorchid, hypogonadal or dystrophic-appearing sons may develop homosexuality or a homosexual pattern behaviour, these abnormalities are seldom to be found in committed homosexuals.

One anorchid male, a committed homosexual, treated from puberty with androgens, wanted testicular prostheses inserted for a better body image and he was always, in his own words, the passive partner. It has been suggested that feminine traits in 5 to 12 year old boys may be fixed if not corrected and their mannerisms may be regarded as phenotypes. Phenotypes associated with homosexuality were once suggested and certain individual types were thought to be more likely. There is no evidence for this nor for an earlier suggestion that constitutional feminism might allow recognition of "latent" homosexuals. There are homosexuals who claim to recognise the condition in younger siblings or relatives, but mostly erroneously. None the less, feminine behaviour patterns in younger boys or masculine ones in girls suggest a defect in the family and may antedate a homosexual disposition.

The characteristics of homosexuals are variable and protean but some confirmed homosexuals deport themselves, both in behaviour and dressing, in a cultural pattern that favours recognition if the pattern is known. Others do not dress out of keeping with their professional image, even in leisure periods or when away in a group staying at a motel or similar. Contrary to some belief, the husky athletic and aggressively masculine and mesomorphic male is as likely to be a homosexual as the average male, and in some situations more so. In others, the effeminate and elegant young male is no more likely than any other but simply represents the behaviour pattern of his peer group. The tough sado-masochistic male, whether well educated or barely literate, may equally be homosexually disposed. To argue that group sports, with rough body contact, deter the sexually disposed, or may prevent development of this disposition is not correct. Indeed, a football scrum may stimulate some and allow the clandestine contact that they crave.

In certain areas, a work identity may make a person suspect, often unjustifiably, but the homosexual person because of the very talents that relate to his role-playing may and does gravitate to some vocations. It is not unusual to know that a group of people employed in certain areas or because of professional qualifications have a common disposition. On occasions, a broken engagement or a marriage between professional people that failed, with unusual bitterness and hurt in the woman, may be suspect. From other cultures and periods, as well as from contemporary personal understanding, there are sufficient autobiographies and biographies to suggest that typing of the disposition is not possible without personal history or disclosure. Often, mannerisms reveal a committed disposition but, retrospectively, most of these have been acquired, and sometimes unconsciously, in their milieu. These may be most obvious in a self-conscious setting when in public gaze, or under stress, and on meeting someone whom they once knew mostly before their disposition was likely to be known. The behaviour in some areas is obviously very dramatic.because they wish to be recognised, but this is quite different from the signals and other recognition signs flashed in pick-up areas. Such behaviour is not the usual.

At times, in the presence of male homosexuals, females who may not know their disposition, which can even be bisexual, become uncomfortable and react strongly to the behaviour described as fawning or pawing.[26] They may describe goose pimples, unease[27] or sheer attack.[28] Males may also react to female homosexuals with unease, and this without being forewarned, sometimes becoming abusive or physically aggressive. At times, then, in both contexts of social contact, there is a total ignorance of the disposition of the other which has made sheer attack or aggression harder to accept. The sociological study by Hauser[29] of an English setting, not strictly applicable to local situations (though similar studies confirm the pattern for other social groups), indicates the variety of personality and phenotype involved. Some transvestite homosexuals, and not only those who dress for the big occasion, but who constantly cross-dress, appear so womanly that they are not detected. Some of these "play games" and may be roughly treated should they allow the games to go too far, particularly if found out during sexual play with an apparent heterosexual male.

In terms of causation, it can be emphasized that there is no confusion with genital sex. Denials of physical sexuality (males hating their penis and scrotum, females their breasts and menstrual losses etc.) are characteristic of transsexuals or gender dysphoria. The confusion arises with erotic desires and so the disposition is established. It would seem, briefly, that stress, psychological or nurture factors are paramount and predispose the individual to become a homosexual or to acquire a homosexual disposition. Thus, the disposition is acquired. It is not innate or inborn; it is a matter of choice, with the choice being less for some than others. The ethology of the disposition[30] stresses that some cultures make the choice easier for those who have the inclination to commit themselves to this way of life, but other cultures, because of prevenient strictures and commands, make it more difficult. Christian believers in the past, firmly adhering to biblical insights, have said, "it is not a gift of God or of grace". This produces intense guilt for the troubled in a Christian community.

This is the point at which, in our attention to causative factors, a brief discussion of iatrogenic homosexuality - that thought to originate with the physician - would seem appropriate. The frailty of male psycho-sexuality is evident and it appears easier for natural processes to make a male than female. Matched pairs of hermaphrodites suggest how heavily weighted is the contribution of the post-natal phase of gender-identity differentiation. It has been suggested above that maiden aunts of a certain temperament have succeeded in introducing a dysphoria. Equally some lonely fathers have not succeeded in stabilizing the female gender of their only child, a daughter. The hypospadic male brought up as a girl has been termed an instance of iatrogenic homosexuality but this would only be so if the genetic and organ sex were dominant to the personality, which they should not be.

The parent facing the problem of a hermaphrodite or pseudo-hermaphrodite child that is to be brought up as a specified sex must never have any doubt or ambiguity as to whether the child is a boy or girl. The parents must understand what is happening in order to communicate with the child so that the child can respond with trust as he is instructed according to his understanding. It is evident for these situations that sex of assignment and rearing can be discordant for gender identity in a twin pair. The physician must understand existentially the significance of this, and the parents must never doubt because, if they do, then so does the child. This can happen even for someone with a homogeneous sex of personality structure, as for example the father and mother who keep assignment, rearing and gender identity, when remarks threaten the constantly and verbally doubting their boy's true manhood. Situations have arisen in the past where the penis has been ablated (in a circumcision accident) or a microphallus was present and the boy has been corrected for life as a female. Their gender identity has differentiated discordantly with their chromosomal and organ sex (prenatal sex). The pedantically extreme may term this homosexuality, but such usage must then be heavily qualified.

40

These facts stress that the primary or basic origins of homosexuality, bisexuality, and heterosexuality lie in the developmental period of the postnatal era, especially infancy and childhood. Then,pubertal hormones bring the dispositions to full or modified expression.

There appear to be no hormonal associations specific to homosexuality. Although homosexual males are unlikely to be 47, XXY or 47, XYY, these two groups may have a higher incidence of homosexuality in some selected groups and the 47, XYY males a higher incidence of sex offenders.[31] Three publications[32]are often quoted to suggest that androgen levels are lower in homosexual males. The groups are small and perhaps only the last publication suggests that among homosexual males there may be some who have testicular abnormalities, including lower than normal plasma testosterone levels and low sperm counts. Gonadotrophin levels have also been reported by Kolodny et. al. (1972).[33]

That some homosexual males may have testicular abnormalities seems certain but this is not a constant association. Others have well-defined features of androgen action and male type baldness. Those with testicular abnormalities show the parameters of their disorder whether this is an instance of Sertoli only cell, fertile eunuch, Klinefelter's, germ cell failure or tubular degeneration syndromes. Those without testicular abnormalities have normal plasma testosterone (as tested by specific and sensitive isotopic methods) or normal testosterone and other androgens, oestrogens, gonadotrophins and prolactin (as tested by radioimmunoassay methods). Some homosexuals have taken oestrogen and these reduce androgen levels; others have received testosterone, even to the extent of addiction, and the gonadotrophins will be suppressed as by feed-back control. Some feel their powers are waning and seek for added androgen, others have sought oestrogen for relief in their drives. Sperm counts are seldom checked but the actual numbers are dependent upon frequency of masturbation and duration of abstinence. Impotent homosexual males appear to fall into similar groups to their heterosexual peers. The testosterone levels may be low to high normal and gonadotrophin levels may be variously low normal to normal. Some older males worried with waning potency and the fear of loneliness[34]have low testosterone and high gonadotrophin levels, and this pattern has been found in heterosexual males as part of sexual declension.

These results have been collected over some 15 years. However, female homosexuals have been less well studied. Some by appearance are entirely normal-appearing females and others have adopted a masculine mode without being less than female. Some have a polycystic ovary syndrome (with hirsutism and acne, and feel themselves to have unwanted non-feminine characteristics) but this is not a constant association.

In this context, it is significant that oestrogens (ethinyloestradiol) or oestrogenic substances (stilboestrol) reduce sexual drive and urges in some homosexuals who are concerned about the intensity of their urges and have sought relief. Anti-androgen therapy of a different type given to men aware of and troubled by the inappropriateness of the object of their sexual fantasies and activities can limit drives also.[35] However, such anti-androgen and oestrogen therapy does not relieve the psychological aggression of most. The Danish experience would likewise suggest that castration (practised in Denmark for sexual offenders and recividists) can reduce sexual libido but does not significantly affect aggressive behaviour. The anti-androgen, cyproterone acetate has certainly diminished the frequency and intensity of sexual fantasies and behaviour[36] and can reduce hirsutism in women and male transsexuals.

The target population for much of this research derives from overseas penal systems and may not reasonably be applicable to most persons. However, it does suggest that low levels of androgens are not correlated with homosexuality, though the levels may correlate with urges. Androgen levels in otherwise normal males are subject to fluctuation with stress, fatigue, stimulation as well as biological rhythms. It would appear that testosterone at best has a permissive effect in much the same way that cortisol (hydrocortisone, the normal corticosteroid of the human adrenal cortex) can be said to have a permissive effect for bodily functions. Falling levels, as in sexual declension or as the result of alcoholism, may affect the intensity of the homosexual urgings in the same way that heterosexual urgings can be lessened. Addiction to testosterone medication, given parenterally, is understood in a similar way.

These facts suggest inescapably that the homosexual disposition is a reflex of education in its broadest sense and motivations. Perhaps it may be wisest to consider the committed homosexually disposed male and question the patterns of sexual arousal in him. It is necessary to discuss what "turns him on and off". In one sense homosexuality is not the counterpart of heterosexuality (see above, Kinsey report). The arousal mechanisms in most heterosexuality include few intervening variables, which is not to deny their significance.

The variables appear more complicated for homosexuality. Often the homosexual is aroused by stimuli that may be identifiably feminine, as for example a male who resembles a female from his family in some respect or attribute (e.g. facial presentation; also there may be a quicker reaction to males with makeup). Other cues are to be found in skin colour and texture, fat distribution in the areas that are those of secondary sexual locations. Sometimes, it may be legs, hips and legs, or a style of walking. Of course, these may be regarded as hetero-sexual cues, but they are located in homosexual objects or persons, depending upon these impulses. Family relationships are relevant but not strictly causative and homosexuality appears to evolve as an adaptation to heterosexual dysfunction. This appears to be found where the mother is inappropriately intimate (dominant and/or seductive) and the father denigrated (weak and/or hostile) or detached (possibly hostile).

In this background the boy is subjected to a variety of factors within and without the family (psycho-dynamic, sociocultural, biological, situational, etc.) that have subtle temporal, qualitative and quantitative variables. He is often a "sissy" at home and abroad, among his peer group and their girl friends, and with his school teacher. Some teachers fail to help and they and the peer group simply aggravate his maladaptation.

The factors combine to create (1) an impaired gender-identity, (2) a fear of intimate contact with the opposite sex[37] and (3) opportunities for sexual release with members of the same sex. If regarded as an adaptation then homosexuality combines to provide (1) a substitute for heterosexual activity and gratification, (2) a defence against expectations of injury from other males although this may still occur in "beatings-up", and (3) a reparative function structured to strengthen damaged self-esteem and to repair defective interpersonal relationships, especially with males. Within the family, the contributing dynamics cannot be discerned at the time unless there be keen observation of the problems which the dominating mother, the hostile and detached father may be acting out. Sometimes the hostile father is acting out problems he formerly experienced with his own father or a sibling. The dominating mother may remain "more in love" with her own father than her husband or constantly compare her father with her husband, to his detriment.

At times, the erotic stimulus in another male may be seen as a feared symbol of masculine (virile) power or a characteristic of feared males from the past. As with heterosexual arousals, it could be hair, hands, shoulders, perfume etc., but it can also be the large penis or muscular physique of the other. The correlates with masochism and sadism are obvious.

The loss of understanding of the nature of the heterosexual relationship, from arousal to satisfaction, and the introduction of aggression, the need to overpower, have helped many misunderstand its true nature. The other so easily becomes an object rather than another person. For instance, one male is aroused by the possibility of overpowering another person, male or female. He is aggressive and yet overprotective in his attitude to a female, being fearful of rejection; while his satisfaction may be somewhat traumatic for her. His response to males may be variable.

The arousal may come from expressed affection, warmth and interest from another male who may or may not be homosexual. If homosexual, the warmth may be the only reason for contact and, if so, occasion a search for warmth in others. Some may return to a "household" where warmth was once found, as if loneliness and the fear of being alone are the motivating factors, even though they may be rejected to the extent of injury. Others simply wish to be held, to have their breasts or body touched and may not wish for more than mutual masturbation, if that. They require (like some women) contact gratification, but in some cases find anal intromission distressing, and have no real wish to fellate another.

There are situations which facilitate and potentiate sexual arousal in the homosexual as well as precipitating a homosexual-type syndrome in some otherwise heterosexual males. Just as excitement, achievement and high points in life may increase heterosexual activity, so may the same factors increase homosexuality. It is suggested[38] that achievement antagonizes powerful males. To both the committed homosexual and the apparent heterosexual with homosexual problems there are threatening males, albeit irrationally perceived. Sexual acts, whether in fantasy or fact, represent submission and appeasement or defensive strategies. It is believed that for some males integration with a large penis, whether in fellation or anal intromission, produces a sense of masculine well-being. In others, there is simply release of tension, relief and physical satisfaction or happiness. Sexual arousal may simply be a means of perpetuating a dependent relationship, or one likely to be broken, and represents a security measure.

Homosexual panic states tend to occur in apparent heterosexual men but panic activity can occur in the committed homosexual when his existence is threatened. At the same time panic may lead to suicidal attempts or altered behaviour that is alien to a previous life-style.[39] At times, the male whose previous disposition has been homosexual but controlled with careful behaviour will reveal himself by an indiscretion. Whether this is intended or is the result of over-confidence cannot be decided easily. At times, alcohol intake, depression or stress appear to have been factors. At other times, an older man has revealed himself to those in his trust. Sadly, others have revealed themselves in a professional situation where their professional standing guaranteed protection. In both situations younger men have been involved.

Neglecting theory and accepting only description, some come from an apparently normal family background. The father is likely to be a professional man, not of high social standing, and the family has provided a good secondary education for the boys in a prestigious Public School. The son leaving home and entering the business world, where his father has been successful, finds a new world. It is not the apparent world of the homosexual culture criticized by the family but one of warmth, personal expression and a measure of security. He describes his entry into this world as one of "conversion". Previously there were elements of loneliness within a family whose behaviour was patterned towards the opposite sex, having expectations of success and good behaviour for the son. His transition is relatively sudden, as if confirming the subjective poverty of a previous life style. Perhaps, also, he has been seduced by the blatantly sexual tone of so much in contemporary society and culture.

It has been said that a homosexual, with exceptions, is a latent heterosexual. His cues have heterosexual features but he may never have the olfactory awareness of women. When a homosexual desires to be rid of his homosexual identity, the prognosis can only be determined by the

44

strength of his wanting to alter, his will to alter. Some do not want to alter and their attendant problems must be treated on their merits, with sympathy and with an understanding of why the problems concern them. No single cause and effect can be found, and Hatterer[40]summarizes a variety of factors taken from a number of sources to emphasize that it is not enough to study the home from which the homosexual came. Some may wish they could relive their life but realize that they would have to choose a different life style, one without the arousals of the present and sometimes without its attendant worldly success and stimulation.

Should a person succeed in a transition from the homosexual disposition he still has problems. His sustained homosexual consciousness and/or activity throughout his past life have effects upon his present life. It is unlikely that he will ever rid himself totally of his past consciousness. He will have certain vulnerabilities revealed by signs of anxiety or dejection and withdrawal. Heterosexual sexual intercourse cannot be regarded as signifying cure, for it has taken place so often as an act, not as a lasting relationship. Females can still produce blocks for him in non-sexual interactions. Experience of a homosexophilic woman can widen his experience, and may not be so threatening as the managing, competitive, sexually manipulative and sexually demanding but masculine modish woman. The woman who is motherly and perhaps older but insecure through unattractiveness, and the one with undue femininity are undesirable companions. The situation of a committed homosexual male attracted to a committed homosexual female, both of whose sexual urges have waned, is not unknown. This relationship can be permanent, intellectually satisfying and creative without sexual demands and the need to establish a conventional family life.

The Christian believer may appear to have a greater chance of altering his disposition but he still needs to will to alter this, without having to cope also with the critical voices of church believers[41]. He may also be confused by other voices who believe the homosexual life style is not incompatible with a believing committed Christian life style, as a slave of God or a slave of righteousness[42].

Finally homosexuality cannot be considered apart from the insights of many who are not clinicians in the restrictive sense. Gilder[43]takes issue with much of today's current thinking on sexuality and believes men and women commit sexual suicide if they deny their divergent sexuality. It cannot be denied that gay liberation and display (leaving aside the pseudohomosexuals whom the committed eschew) represent a threat to many whose male identities and masculine gender roles are precarious. It is possible that, by reaffirming the sexual differences, education may strengthen the male-female relationship. It is difficult to deny anatomy and, in a sense, anatomy is destiny. Man's very first error was to deny a destiny, and to deny the supremacy of mind-brain over body is also to deny destiny.

*«Acknowledgement is made to the many, who cannot be named, who taught me in their distress and dismay of their homosexuality and trans-sexuality. Those who challenged me with their problems, as they sought support and revealed their inner selves, helped me to understand and, I hope, to care. Those who criticized what they saw as superficial or thoughtless comment on my part made me reconsider much. Those whose presuppositions and way of life differed from mine helped me to understand and sympathize with their responses. I trust no one will feel that I have betrayed a trust or confidence, or twisted their views for my own purposes.»

1 To give one example, an adolescent who sees himself in a dream as being in a homosexual situation may only be reflecting the stresses of establishing a gender or his own sex-identity. He may be fearful during the day that someone may think him a homosexual (particularly if his body is dystrophic) and the dream simply expresses a fear. Waking fear, with or without sleep paralysis, is not unusual. Neither the dream nor the reaction establish homosexuality but they may suggest some conflict.

2 A normal male karyotype is 46, XY and the female 46, XX, with XY and XX being the sex chromosome constitution. A karyotype of 47, XXY does not suggest the male is less male and more female nor does 45, X suggest the female is less so, or more male. A 46, XX male is not to be considered a female male even though no Y chromosome can be defined in any tissue. Indeed, if the sex of rearing of these individuals is normal for the genital sex, they will be identified as individuals of that sex albeit mostly with defective secondary sexual features. All will be hypogonadal in terms of gametogenesis and, as the appropriate gonadal hormones will be deficient with rare exceptions among 47, XXY individuals, they will appear clinically hypogonadal. However, some 46, XY individuals can present as a well-developed female, either with uncommonly or mostly lacking pubic and body hair in addition to a failure of menstruation. They can also appear as undeveloped females. Both would appear to be normal girls at birth, that is grossly hypospadic males, and so the genital sex is female. Reared as girls (see Appendix on Transsexuality) in a normal psychological environment and believing themselves to be female, they would establish a heterosexual relationship with a normal 46, XY male which cannot be considered homosexual except in terms of genetic sex. The normality of such 46, XY girls in all their responses, even to the extent of intense femininity and even although their mother may recognize their abnormality because of her sisters and maiden aunts, is again suggestive of brain-mind dominance. A fully masculinized 46, XX female with penile urethra reared as a boy from birth because of the genital sex (albeit with missing testes) would establish a heterosexual relationship with a normal 46, XX female. Again, the relationship could not be considered homosexual except in terms of genetic sex. These individuals, although able to express their genital and rearing sex, did not have the ability to express their gender sex for they lacked

46

the appropriate genital tracts. In marriage, stresses may arise from their infertility and from ill-considered clinical interpretative comment. Allowing for the obvious - that brevity loses the implications and extensions - interpretations should consider that personality is more substantial than body, or that the body is ephemeral and personality substantial.

[3] The difficulty inherent in this approach is suggested in footnote 2, above. Thus, a hypospadic male (genetic sex) who had regarded herself as a woman, albeit not feminine, felt she could only have intercourse with a female once she was confused by the clinicians and moral tutors who divulged and stressed the given sex. From then on her sexual activity with a normal male was considered homosexual.

[4] Within our own society, some individuals regard mutual masturbation between spouses (man and wife) or a couple (engaged or otherwise) as acceptable. Ovviously, this provides sexual stimulation and response without fear of pregnancy. Likewise, anal intercourse is accepted by some as reasonable within marriage, although the basis for this view may be questioned. Likewise, fellatio is practised by some without concern. Thus, it is possible for a male to deny his homosexuality because similar activity could take place with a spouse or in a heterosexual context.

[5] Schizophrenia is not implied although strong homosexual urges can be an early manifestation of this disorder. Also in some, the other individual may be regarded only as an object for sex without sexual recognition. This can also occur in states of confusion, as from alcohol and drugs or in panic.

[6] E.g. L. J. Hatterer, The Artist in Society, New York: Grove Press, 1965.

[7] Bisexual behaviour may occur in marriage because of ambivalent attitudes. A normal male-female relationship may appear to be present because the husband's clandestine homosexual activity persists sufficiently to take away the heterosexual strain. At other times, homosexual activity reappears only under stress. To contract marriage with a hope that this relationship will redirect sexual urges is almost invariably productive of agony and, finally, causes great suffering for all. Some wives have apparently accepted the husband's bisexual behaviour for the sake of the family in the way that others accept the husband's extramarital affairs, in the absence of which he would not continue the marriage. This behaviour is obviously different from that of an androgenized female with a large phallus, but normal vagina, who was ambivalent because of uncertainty about her sex-identity. Bisexual behaviour can also occur in marriage because the wife continues her prior homosexual relationships although this appears less frequent. Finally, a marriage is possible where both husband and wife follow their own homosexual paths by consent. Most trouble arises from clandestine activity. As intimated above heterosexual marriage should never be recommended to control male homosexual urges; it is frequently disastrous for all, and while the woman receives most sympathy, the man can also be destroyed. At times undue pre-occupation with discomfort in the pudenda, abnormal

sensations and images of organs, and asthenia point to earlier conflicts. For the sake of health the hidden may have to be uncovered. Disorders of potency, loosely defined, are less likely to be a marker of such conflict, but they may be. Rape intercourse in marriage can also indicate such conflicts.

[8] The point can be illustrated by five abbreviated histories. The first two relate to women in their 3rd decade. The first woman was chosen for her work because of her evident femaleness and femininity and was glabrous skinned. The second woman, although definitely female, was rather mesomorphic, physically active and aggressive with some hirsutism, acne and irregular menstruation. Both had steady boy friends, the former being engaged; both men revealed their homosexuality by discarding the women. Both men suggested that their attractiveness depended upon their masculinity. This was revealing because a normal heterosexual male would not react to the first woman other than as very female. Obviously, the friend was cued by a physical feature that became obvious later - her boylike body, that is small breasts. Both women developed real fears about their own identity, and, in particular, their own sex identity, from which they only recovered with difficulty. The third woman was somewhat older, highly intelligent and had married a man of lower attainments after a brisk affair. She became pregnant on the wedding night. Before the child was born her husband left her and his homosexuality was revealed to her, although it had been well known by others. Problems of identity were considerable for her, and it did not help her to know that alcohol had enabled him to behave heterosexually. He did provide for his son but never wanted to see him. The fourth woman could not understand how her husband could leave her with a 20 month old son and flat with his friend; she felt that, no matter how much it would hurt him to return, the son whom he had adored would bring him home. Finally, a young man, already troubled by gynaecomastia and poor sex identity following a threat of and indeed an attempted homosexual rape, became acutely depressed because of his social image. He felt he was a homosexual and would be recognized as such.

[9] Brutality, or sadism, against young boys has reflected the homosexual conflicts of some. One instance was a young officer who had great difficulty in controlling his violence when interrogating boys for minor offences. This was regarded as sick behaviour by most. The behaviour of another couple was regarded as sick also and bizarre. One had his rectum resected following a stricture, after a tropical venereal disease. He was provided with a permanent colostomy. His partner used this for intromission by way of artificial anal intercourse, and subjected it to much trauma.

[10] At this stage, the potential sex may fail to develop if the adrenal cortex and gonads cannot hydroxylate steroids appropriately. Failure of androgen synthesis means lack of male differentiation and the individual appears to be a female. Likewise, if androgen action is inadequate anomalies in the differentiation of the external genitalia may occur. At the most extreme, there can be normal androgen production but the tissues do not respond to an androgen. This occurs either

48

because the hormone is not reduced to a tissue active form or because tissue receptors are at fault. The result is a grossly hypospadic male appearing as a female. Contrariwise, the adrenal gland may synthesize sufficient androgen to produce an anomaly in the differentiation of the female external genitalia so that at the extreme a genetic female may appear as a male with absent testes (indeed, two successful boy athletes were really pseudo-hermaphrodites of this type; but their success, when older, would be doubtful and is not known). More frequently, such unfortunate persons appear as androgenized (masculinized) females who, before treatment was available, were sometimes made more comfortable socially by reassignment surgery.

[11] There is an Indian group who have known for some centuries their inability to differentiate males with split scrotums at this stage from females. They know that they must await the revelation of pubertal development. Names are chosen appropriately for those afflicted by this in-born error of development, which is due to an enzymatic deficiency.

[12] A grossly hypospadic male is more likely to be brought up as a female but can be brought up as a male. Naturally, corrective surgery is required and there will be conflicts because of the lag between his body appearances and mental development. The male who is brought up as a female may have problems at puberty particularly if a testis migrates at that time, if phallic development takes place, if hirsutism is undue or if breasts fail to develop.

[13] Cf. J. Money and A. A. Ehrnhardt, Man and Woman, Boy and Girl, Baltimore: The Johns Hopkins Press, 1972.

[14] In some groups, denigration of femaleness so that females appear less female than in parallel groups is usual and does not imply a situation other than normal. Dressing in unisex clothes is then usual. In other situations, male clothes are worn because they are simply more durable or suitable. Denigration of maleness may occur in some groups without inordinate emphasis, both sexes appearing unisex and perhaps more of one than the other. However in males emphasis of femaleness in dressing and presentation may be deliberate affectation or indicative of variable homosexuality. Cross dressing may be a fetishism or a failure to accept sexuality. However, at times, the thrill and excitement of being other than what you are, with others deluded, seems the basis for some social cross dressing and has no erotic features. The appearance of heterosexual traits, e. g. significant gynaecomastia or failure of breast development, in a society where adulation of the breast or its worship is usual, may lead to sex identity problems and insecurity. Equally, inadequate size of the penis either in its non-erected or erected state (whether objectively or subjectively judged does not matter) will arouse doubts of masculinity (sic virility) for many. These doubts are likely to be reinforced by female scorn as when such a male seeks a 'call' girl or attempts a relationship with a physically aggressive and demanding woman.

[15] Hirsutism in females, and it may be entirely normal female hirsutism, arouses doubts as to femininity. These are mostly abetted by cosmetic advertising. Absence of testes may have tragic

consequences and prostheses are essential for an adequate body image from early life with appropriate hormonal replacement. Without an adequate body image or a healthy concept of what is normal, including the accepted range of variability within the normal, neither sex will be at ease.

16 Thus R. W. Goy, "Experimental Control of Psychosexuality Phil. Trans. Royal Soc. London, B259, pp. 149-162.

17 F. J. Money and A. A. Ehrhardt, op. cit.

18 Thus R. W. Goy and D. A. Goldfoot, 1974, variously cited, see J. M. Reinisch, "Effects of Prenatal Hormone Exposure on Physical and Psychological Development in Humans and Animals", in E. J. Sachar (ed.). Hormones Behaviour and Psychopathology, New York; Raven Press, 1976.

19 Excessive clitoral development merits early amputation to relieve problems with body image both for the child and parents. Clitoridectomy, as practised by some native peoples, has a different significance which may or may not be adequately founded. Some girls have had, even recently, clitoridectomy to abate sexual tensions. In this regard, a girl with 45, X constitution having clitoral enlargement merits similar treatment especially if she lacks so much that is socially feminine, but also to ensure appropriate body image.

20 One young male who attempted intercourse with younger school girls unsuccessfully had erotic tattoos over his arms. More distressing is an instance of a young hypogonadal woman, recorded elsewhere, who had "pay as you enter" as a tattoo over the mons veneris which would be lacking hair. An older commentator (The Song of Solomon 8:8-9) was aware of discordant responses to such a problem.

21 See Appendix 2; Transsexuality.

22 Thus C. Fisher, J. Gross and J. Zuch, "Cycle of Penile Erection Synchronous with Dreaming (REM) Sleep", Arch. Gen. Psychiatry, Vol. 12, 1965, pp. 29-45.

23 Thus P. D. MacLean, "Brain Mechanisms of Primal Sexual Functions & Related Behaviour", in M. Sandler and G. L. Gessa (eds.), Sexual Behaviour: Pharmacology and Biochemistry, New York: Raven Press, 1975.

24 Thus N. Shainess, "Authentic Feminine Erotic Responses", in M. Sandler and G. L. Gessa, op. cit., pp. 283-289.

25 See, for example, P. Brown (ed.) Radical Psychology, London: Tavistock Publications, 1973.

26 The description of pawing may seem unusual but derives from experiences in hairdressing salons, exclusive dress shops etc. Males have also complained of unnecessary body contact in similar situations, not forgetting schoolboys. In this context, a group of young women did not care for a shop where the very efficient, unisex males or "lovelies" seemed to gain pleasure from their close physical attentions. However, their reaction could have equally been similar to another (see note 18).

27 This has been described by women therapists attending male homosexuals in a nursing type situation and from observation of behaviour in some vocational areas. It can occur without any forewarning. The therapist's reaction to a male homosexual who was the secretary for

a call-girl service (rather like a eunuch of the past) was distressing, and unfortunately introduced complications for his care.

[28] To illustrate, a university student could not understand why her tutor, to whom she warmed and whom she patently respected for his professional competence and patient care, unexplainably and rather brutally castigated her in a small group tutorial. It appeared that he, a committed and avowed homosexual, had been threatened by her and she was very warmly feminine. His reaction appeared uncontrolled; he later apologized to the group. In another instance, a woman was terrified by a physician who appeared to abuse and denigrate her when she consulted him. Unwittingly her neurotic responses aroused reactions that were stronger than usual as he had some difficulty with hysterical responses in women.

[29] R. Hauser, The Homosexual Society, London: The Bodley Head, 1962.

[30] See J. Money and A. A. Ehrhardt, op. cit., for a brief review of customs.

[31] Thus J. Money, C. Wiedeking, P. A. Walker and D. Gain, "Combined Antiandrogenic and Counselling Program for Treatment of 46, XY and 47, XYY Sex Offenders, in E. V. Sachar, op. cit.

[32] M. Margolese, "Homosexuality: A New Endocrine Correlate" Hormones and Behaviour, Vol. I, 1970, pp. 151-155. J. A. Loraine, A. A. A. Ismail, D. A. Adamopoulos and G. Dove, "Endocrine Function in Male and Female Homosexuals", Brit. Med. J., Vol. 4, 1970, pp. 406-409. R. C. Kolodny, W. H. Masters, J. Hendryx and G. Toro, "Plasma Testosterone and Semen Analysis in Male Homosexuals", New England J. Med., 285, 1971, pp. 1170-1174.

[33] R. C. Kolodny, L. S. Jacobs, W. H. Masters, G. Toro and W. H. Daughaday, "Plasma Gonadotrophins and Prolactin in Male Homosexuals", Lancet, Vol. 2, 1972, pp. 17-19.

[34] Impotence and waning sexual libido can be most distressing for an older homosexual person. Visits from his friends can become less and he has less inclination to seek them out so that he faces loneliness and sometimes real despair. Resort to the panacea of alcohol may aggravate the problem. The alcoholic homosexual may also become impotent from alcoholic liver disease. The older lesbian may well face loneliness but more often like her heterosexual sisters has greater personal resources.

[35] Thus J. Money et al., 1976, op. cit.

[36] A. J. Cooper, A. A. A. Ismail, A. L. Phonjoo and D. L. Lore, "Antiandrogen (Cyproterone Acetate) Therapy in Deviant Hypersexuality", British Psychiatry, 120, 1972, pp. 58-64.

[37] Some young males superficially appear to say that they started sex with another male rather than risk unwanted pregnancies in girls, or that it was better this way. With the advent of the anovulant pill this seems less cogent. Perhaps this is really an aspect of pseudohomosexuality.

[38] I. Bieber, "Homosexual Dynamics in Psychiatric Crises", Amer. J. Psychiatry, 128, 1972, p. 10.

[39] The covert homosexual of professional standing, whose background

is quite well respected, may emerge into a group that is alien to his
background, aesthetic tastes and intellectual standard. His subsequent
reaction may be remorse, dejection and sense of self-betrayal. Homosexual panic may take place in a normal otherwise stable and natural
family. Often there is a disappearance with subsequent denial or
bluffing over its significance. The tension for the family in such a
deception, although its real significance is unknown, is traumatic.
When the significance becomes apparent, the stress for the family
can be more than it can cope with. There may then be rejection of
the father and husband, bringing its own disasters.

[40] L. J. Hatterer, Changing Homosexuality in the Male, New York:
McGraw-Hill Book Company, 1970.

[41] Thus G. Charles, "The Church and the Homosexual", in G. R.
Collins (ed.), The Secrets of Our Sexuality, Waco, Texas: Word Books
Publisher, 1976.

[42] Troy Perry, "God Loves Me Too", in W. D. Oberholtzer (ed.),
Is Gay Good?, Westminster, Philadelphia, 1971. D. S. Bailey,
Homosexuality and the Western Christian Tradition, London: Longman,
Green and Co., 1955.

[43] Gilder, G. F., Sexual Suicide, London: Millington, 1973.

APPENDIX 1
BIBLICAL INSIGHTS ON HOMOSEXUALITY

'Who are you to pass judgment on the servant of another?
It is before his own master that he stands or falls.'
                                        Paul, Saul of Tarsus.
FOR the Christian believer who is also a clinician, homosexuality is a
qualitative aspect of behaviour. The explicit biblical insight is binding
for the believer. What society, the state, the church and clinicians have
to say on their own behalf is interesting, sometimes illuminating, but not
binding. The Bible construes homosexuality in the context of sexuality.
The creation insight shows man as male and female (Genesis 1:27) and a
male-female sexual relationship is established which is called good.
Thus, it would seem that the faculty of maleness and femaleness was
given for this facility of sexual relationship and the differentiation of
female from male was specific (Genesis 2:18 et seq.). In this regard,
the anatomical differences are construed as the faculty for a specific
purpose of genital intercourse. The male-female union was regarded
by both Christ and Paul as a norm established of God for Christian man
or, previously, God's covenant people.

It would seem that any attitude against homosexuality as a life style
or an alternative for a Christian has to be weighted against the biblical
view of sexuality.

Indeed, the male-female relationship is a parable of our need of God, and marriage is a parable of a preparation for communion with God. The Bible does not regard the homosexual as a special class of sinner but a person for whom Christ also died, a victim of sin and a sinful society, who can be reconciled to God through Christ. The Christian believer must not have his thinking conformed to the pattern of the world but have a transformed mind (Romans 12:2), without which sweet reasonableness may be receptive of worldly attitudes. The measurement of grading or behaviour may lead to a disregard of absolutes.

APPENDIX 2
TRANSSEXUALITY

A transsexual is by assumption not a homosexual. Nonetheless, transsexuality may logically be regarded as the extreme disposition of homosexuality, or a circumscribed psychosis. Mostly, male to female transsexuals are called to mind by the designation but female to male are known, albeit less commonly. Historically, the gender dysphoria is well known as 'eonism' after the famed Chevalier d'Eon. Historically, the technique of castrating young boys and forcing a vagina was known. This procedure was crude and septic and carried a considerable mortality, the survivors becoming 'women'. The customs of many native peoples allowed transsexuals a place in their society, often honoured without such surgery.

Transsexuality may be defined as gender misidentification with, for the male, a life-long preference for the female role predicated on the conviction of belonging to the female sex. This conviction is held incontrovertibly and held against the obvious male anatomy and genitalia, before and after puberty with its secondary sexual development. The genitalia produce revulsion or are hated and there can be attempts at self castration. He rationally denies homosexuality but any relationship must be with a male, preferably a normal heterosexual male. He regards sexual intercourse with a woman as "homosexual and unnatural" but overt sexual activity is often minor. Accepting that he is a female, who by an error in development has physically developed as a male, he soon cross-dresses (some model clothes and, after mammoplasty, swimming costumes; some work as female strippers). Adopting a full female role, sex-reassignment surgery is sought. The decision to operate is determined by absence of psychosis (for someone to believe a uterus and ovaries could be found, with a possibility of pregnancy later, is unreal and rarely stated), fetishism and overt homosexuality. There must be an ability to live as a woman and security in that role at the appropriate cultural and social level (some have "married", setting up their home before operation). Not all seek sexual intercourse with a male subsequently and some remain unmarried in a satisfactory female role; some have a disturbed life.

The satisfaction of a "married" life confirms for some the worth of surgery but an inability to adopt a child becomes a tragedy for some.

The aetiology is uncertain but in one group only one 47, XXY and one 47, XYY male have been found. Their hormonal parameters were upset by prior oestrogen therapy, often at a high dosage. This oestrogen was generally obtained without medical advice. Thus, testes are atrophic when the penis is carried retroflexed between the thighs (the scrotal folds then superficially resemble labia). It is noteworthy that examination of the genitalia is almost invariably distressing.

A practical problem relates to the possibility of a transsexual being a homosexual, or vice versa, assuming a delineation is accepted and can be made.

Does a transitional phase exist? Should a homosexual transvestite with worrying guilt attitudes, who wants reassignment surgery and can give rationalizations for his transsexuality, be accepted pragmatically as a transsexual? It has seemed that many transsexuals from an early age regard themselves as other than male and have been so treated by their peer group who react to them as females. However, some have anal intercourse, fantasizing that it is vaginal. Most reject this as "unnatural". The family background may suggest those factors noted for the homosexual but some have been fashioned as girls by the family or relatives acting as parents.

The female to male transsexual is less frequent. There are no chromosomal abnormalities and most have felt themselves to be different from their peer group at an early age. Some have been fashioned as males by the family or relatives. They do not regard a sexual relationship with a female as homosexual. There may have been a child from a marriage to establish their normal femaleness, although pregnancy may have been forced upon them. Psychosis should not be evident but neurotic or existential tensions are helped when, what they feel themselves to be, is made more likely by hormonal therapy. The tensions of these transsexuals have not always been fully appreciated and the hurt, which arises from lack of sympathy, may be tragic. The "passing phase" is often most difficult. Reassignment surgery has been less successful but femaleness should be eradicated. Most prefer beards which help their masculine image and acceptance. "Marriage" can be happy and satisfying with an established home. The desire for an AID pregnancy in their "wife" is often the climax for the social recognition of their "maleness".

PART 2: A BIBLICAL PERSPECTIVE

INTRODUCTION

IT is only comparatively recently that the Christian Church has begun to respond to the new ways of asking questions about human sexuality which were brought into clearest focus by the Kinsey Reports. As our chronicle of debate attempted to show (chapter 1), any discussion of homosexuality has to come to terms with the fact that these questions are being discussed and lived out in a constantly changing scene. And the Church is involved in these changes in at least the following ways.

In the first place, the Church is needing to come to terms with the fact that for a variety of reasons the setting of sexual ethics within the ethics of marriage and the family is now being widely questioned and modified. The separation of the relational and procreative aspects to sexual intercourse (largely made possible through the wide availability of contraceptives) means that 'sex' is increasingly being isolated from 'marriage' and affirmed as a positive good in its own right (at best) or used as a commodity (at worst). Furthermore, when so much of the rootless depersonalised state of our collectivized society makes for the 'trivialisation of human encounter' ('which in the name of freedom encourages the minimum of engagement with the maximum haste, and the maximum disengagement, as in premarital experimentation and divorce, with the minimum of effort in the presence of personal difficulties')[1] there is in many a growing longing to find personal meaning and sense of fulfilment in interpersonal relationships. When this is coupled with the hypersexualised context of much of our modern living, with an increasingly neurotic fixation on 'sex' as a commodity, sexual intercourse comes to be thought the sine qua non of a fully meaningful relationship. It is in this context that Christians are attempting to articulate their understanding of human beings as fully sexual beings, of the beauty and richness possible in human interpersonal relationships of love, and of the appropriateness of different ways of relating as sexual beings in different contexts.

In the second place, the Church is needing to be alert to the fact that in a culture which is dominated by a quest for material pleasure and personal happiness, the attempt to articulate an ethic in terms of biblical principles and the will of God is often unfashionable at best, or open to the charge of 'hostile to pleasure and fulfilment' at worst. The Church is needing to find a way of acknowledging and affirming the rightful place of sexual pleasure in appropriate contexts, without falling into the hedonistic trap of stressing pleasure at the expense of

55

respecting personal wholeness and the nature of human being as created in the image of the eternal God. What follows is based on the belief that human life is ultimately fulfilled and satisfied in the enjoyment of the fellowship of the Creator, and that his will for human life articulated in biblical principles, is not only in accord with his own character, but makes for human blessing and fulfilment in the fullest sense. In the Church's discussion of homosexuality, however, we need also to keep in mind the fact that the attempt to live by biblical principles has apparently led to two very negative and shameful results: first, the fact that the majority in the Church has virtually ignored any sense of constructive mission to the homosexual minority, whom it seems, they would often have preferred to go away and leave them alone; and second, the fact of 'homophobia', the term used by homosexual people to describe the fear and hatred with which majority society has all to often regarded homosexual people.

A third area of change, as we pointed out in Chapter 1, has been caused by an uncertainty within the Church about the proper use of the Bible itself. There are two sides to this uncertainty. The first, influentially illustrated by Sherwin Bailey's important work (which we discuss at length later), argues that the traditional interpretation of the Bible on the question of homosexuality has been wrong. The second, followed by some who do and some who do not accept Dr. Bailey's exegesis, says: the traditional understanding of the Bible's teaching may have been right, but that is not the way we now make ethical decisions. This second approach may be illustrated by reference to the review of Dr. R. Moss's booklet Christians and Homosexuality in Gay Christian (Sept. 1978).

> Underlying the thinking of Mr. Moss and others who share his position on homosexuality, is a view of the authority of the Bible that believes the message of God has been preserved in a verbal form with substantial accuracy, and the canonical books of the Old and New Testaments must be regarded as wholly trustworthy, historically as well as in matters of faith and doctrine.

This viewpoint is then set in opposition to a 'second view which allows for the critical and historical study of the Bible over the last hundred years...we are not to regard the Bible primarily as a standard to which we must conform in all questions arising in our life'.

The following chapters of this Study are written from the conviction that critical and historical study is not incompatible with the authority of the Bible (cf. C/E Article VI) nor with the binding nature of its moral obligation on the Christian conscience (cf. C/E Article VII), and from the further conviction that the Christian ethic is primarily one of allegiance, a response of obedient love to the love of the Lawgiver. It is an attempt to contribute to the debates on the subject of homosexuality by articulating the implications both for homosexual people and also for the Christian community of a biblical perspective on these important issues. As we noted at the close of chapter 1, the existence and teaching of Christian Homophile movements do offer a challenge to other Christians who think in terms of the traditional Christian approach to these questions. As we summarily said there, the challenge is a fourfold one; its four points will form the basis for our following chapters.

First, it is a challenge to the traditional view that the homosexual disposition is an abnormal condition representing a deviation from God's norm for human sexuality. Secondly, it is a challenge to the traditional view that homosexual acts are immoral and sinful; a challenge, in other words, to the traditional norms for sexual behaviour; even a questioning, perhaps, whether there are any such norms, and whether any expression of human sexual behaviour can be denied to be positively moral if it falls under the rubric of personal love. Thirdly, and related to this, it is a challenge to consider again, and to reassess, the Scriptural passages which have traditionally been understood to condemn unreservedly all sexual behaviour between members of the same sex as contrary to the will of God. And fourthly, it is a challenge to the mainline Churches at the level of fellowship: how is the Christian church to respond at the level of Christian fellowship (which includes Church discipline) to those of a homosexual orientation who engage in behaviour which has traditionally been understood to be sinful and under divine judgement? Even if on all other counts the traditional view of homosexual behaviour is upheld, the existence of Christian homophile movements expresses a claim and need for fellowship, acceptance and support for those of a homosexual orientation, and poses the question whether an attitude which creates 'fear of rejection and recrimination' is the only appropriate response.

This fourfold challenge is a strong one, probing, as we have said, to the heart of the whole meaning of human sexual identity, and requiring that the Church either rethinks or reaffirms with clearer understanding, a Christian sexual morality which deals adequately with the existence of the homosexual condition, with the biblical norms for sexual behaviour, and with the place of homosexuals within the Christian fellowship.

Personal morality for the homosexual ultimately centres around two questions: Can a person choose his/her sexual orientation? and Can a person choose what he/she does with his/her sexual orientation? These questions are relevant to all four aspects of the Christian homophile challenge as we have outlined it.

Two further important distinctions need now to be clarified. First, by no means all relationships of loving affection between members of the same sex are necessarily 'homosexual' relationships in the sense that they involve men or women whose sexual preference is for their own sex. As Sherwin Bailey comments in his discussion of David and Jonathan:

Any relationship between two persons of the same sex is, strictly speaking, a homosexual relationship, and an affectionate regard entertained by a man for another man, or a woman for another woman, is likewise homosexual. But those who attach a homosexual significance to the intimate friendship between David and Jonathan either imply (against all the facts) that both were inverts (which the Old Testament belies by representing them plainly as normal heterosexual men who married - David polygynously - and had children), or insinuate that they gave their 'love' physical expression in coital acts, of which there is no evidence whatsoever. Against all such unfounded surmises it must be insisted, as Ellis says, that 'there is nothing to show that such a relationship was sexual' in the colloquial sense of the word.[2]

We need to be able to affirm the importance and richness of loving affection between members of the same sex, recognising also that some physical expression of that affectation is sometimes appropriate, (and recognising also that the extent to which such expression is publicly acceptable is often defined by culture and social custom), without any implication being given that such affection is necessarily related to sexual arousal or involves any genital expression. We all relate to one another (members of the same and of opposite sexes) as sexual beings, and relationships of love and affection with members of the same and the opposite sex are deeply involved in what it means to be human. The point at issue in discussion of the morality of sexual behaviour is the appropriateness and legitimacy, or otherwise, of genital expression (and physical demonstrations of affection related to genital expression) in different contexts.

Secondly - as will emerge more clearly during the course of our later discussion - there is a crucially important distinction to be maintained between orientation, inclination and preference on the one hand, and behaviour - including intention to behave - on the basis of that preference, on the other hand. In much current literature, the term 'homosexual' has been used both for the orientation over which there may not be conscious choice, and for the behaviour pattern of a person, in which personal moral choice is almost always significant, and it has not always been clear whether the first only, or both together, are being asserted by it. We shall use the term 'homophile' to refer to a person of homosexual orientation, that is whose sexual preferences are directed towards a member or members of the same sex, but of whom no statement is being made concerning their sexual behaviour; and we shall use the terms 'homosexual acts' or 'homosexual behaviour' to refer to those physical expressions of homosexual preference which are related to deliberate sexual arousal. (Use of such 'clinical' terminology is an attempt at clarification; it is not a denial of the love and warmth which can be present in people or behaviour so described). It is very important in attempting to articulate a Christian ethic to maintain the proper moral distinctions between orientation and preference, desires, temptations, intentions and acts. That such distinctions are of peculiar importance in any discussion of homosexuality will become evident in the following chapters which explore this fourfold challenge to the Christian tradition.

NOTES

[1] Cf. Jack Dominian, Proposals for a New Sexual Ethic, (Darton Longman and Todd, 1977), p. 69.

[2] D. Sherwin Bailey, Homosexuality and the Western Christian Tradition, (Longmans, 1955), p. 56, quoting H. Ellis, Studies in the Psychology of Sex (1918)[2] ii. p. 10.

3. IS HOMOSEXUALITY A 'NATURAL' ORIENTATION?

IN his book We Speak For Ourselves[1] Jack Babuscio makes the point strongly that a great deal of the unhappiness and despair experienced by the homophile community is the result of what is felt to be hostility from the social majority, and in particular from the refusal by the majority to regard the homosexual condition as a 'natural' one. He says:

> It is as a direct result of Society's failure to accept homosexuality as a legitimate variation of the sexual drive, that the gay person's principal problem becomes one of finding an acceptable identity within a hostile environment.[2]

Without elaborating, we note that the elision from 'failure to accept' in the first line of the quotation to 'hostile environment' in the last line, is not a necessary one. Babuscio goes on to say that the argument that homosexuality is 'unnatural' has no rational standing[3] and he disagrees with the traditional viewpoint that 'heterosexual behaviour' is 'the norm'.[4] How is a Christian seeking a biblical perspective on these questions to weigh these increasingly common affirmations?

Certainly the view that homosexual behaviour is 'unnatural' has a long pedigree. In Plato's Laws, the Athenian speaker declares that the pleasure of heterosexual intercourse is granted 'in accordance with nature', whereas homosexual pleasure is 'contrary to nature' and a 'crime caused by failure to control the desire for pleasure'.[5] Likewise, the Testaments of the Twelve Patriarchs which gives a specifically sexual interpretation of the 'fornication of Sodom',[6] urges 'my children' to recognise... 'in all created things, the Lord who made all things, that ye be not as Sodom, which changed the order of nature'.[7] So also Philo and Josephus (see references in Appendix to chapter 5 by R. T. Beckwith), refer to homosexual behaviour as 'contrary to nature'. But in biblical theology, 'natural' is used in a specific way. In his paper 'Is it a natural alternative?'[8] O. M. T. O'Donovan rightly points out that for a Christian thinker, claims about 'nature' are not to be separated from the doctrine of Creation. To ask whether homosexuality is 'natural' is to ask whether God made it. 'While in one sense, everything that exists is made by God, in another important sense, Christian theology distinguishes between what God created in the first instance, and what has happened subsequently'... 'Whereas everything created by God is good, good without qualification, much of what he allows, though it serves his good ends, is in itself problematic or tragic.

So then, to ask whether homosexuality is 'natural' is also to ask whether it is essentially good. It is not enough simply to say that since people with a homosexual disposition do exist, and since they have not chosen this disposition themselves, 'the Lord has done it.' We must know in what respect He has done it. Is it part of his good creation deed, the gift of being and order which precedes all that we are and do? Has mankind received humanity from God's hand, asks O'Donovan, already divided into homosexual and heterosexual? From the biblical perspective, the answer has to be 'no'. Commenting on the 'primeval history' of the early chapters of Genesis, O'Donovan says:

> Almost all the significant differences among men, racial, cultural and linguistic, are there represented as supervening after the Fall. Only one difference is recorded before the Fall, the difference between male and female. The point of this ordering is to establish distinct evaluations. The difference between the sexes is natural, part of God's good creation and of positive value for the human race, while the other differences are to a greater or lesser degree ambiguous. Differences of language, to take a clear example, are a sign of God's judgement (Gen 11); differences between slave race and master race arise out of an ancestor's curse (Gen 9); differences between agriculturalist and pastoral nomad provoke the first murder (Gen 4). Of course we must add that the natural difference may be corrupted to become an occasion of exploitation, and that the tragic difference may be redeemed and become an occasion of reconciliation. But the point remains: the one difference is essentially good, the others problematic.[9]

The fundamental 'creation pattern' for human sexuality is focussed in Gen 1.27: 'So God created man in his own image: male and female he created them'. Although the author of Genesis 1 may well not have been aware of the crucial distinction (to which we referred earlier) between behaviour and orientation his theology of sexuality is the presupposition upon which other biblical authors who it seems (see chapter 5) certainly were aware of the distinction, base their ethical teaching. This verse is taken alongside Gen 2.24 as a basis in creation for Jesus' teaching on the meaning of marriage in Matt. 19.4-6 and Mark 10.6-9. And Paul, in his development of the analogy between human marriage and the relationship between Christ and the church presupposes the normative nature of heterosexual marriage. Furthermore, (as we shall discuss in more detail in chapter 5), every biblical reference to homosexual behaviour comes in a condemnatory context, and Paul in Romans 1 specifically chooses homosexual behaviour as his first example of behaviour "against nature" (see chapter 5) characteristic of a culture founded on idolatry which rejects the norms of the Creator, and as a mark in that culture of the judgement of God (Rom 1. 18-32).

From the point of view of what is 'natural' to God's good creation, homosexuality (alongside of course other sexual distortions characteristic of those of heterosexual disposition) has therefore to be viewed as a distortion and an abnormality.

61

Helmut Thielicke comments:

> The fundamental order of the creation and the created
> determination of the sexes make it appear justifiable to
> speak of homosexuality as a 'perversion' - in any case if
> we begin with the understanding that this term implies no
> moral depreciation whatsoever, and that it is used purely
> theologically in the sense that homosexuality is in every
> case not in accord with the order of creation.[10]

His qualification of definition is important, because 'perversion' has in
common currency a perjorative sense which Thielicke does not intend.
To use the term 'perversion' raises the question as to the norm against
which it is to be defined, and we need to be clear that Thielicke (rightl
defines the norms for human sexuality from the doctrine of creation (a
not from psychological or emotional subjective desires, nor from the
reproductive purpose of sexual intercourse). Nonetheless, the value i
the term, if it can be used without perjorative overtones, is the pointe
to the fact that in the light of God's good creation, homosexuality is no
merely a statistical deviation from a majority orientation and behaviou
pattern, but an abnormality of a different kind: a distorted sexuality.
There is not merely something different, but something questionable.

Thielicke then distinguishes two further important points. First, th
'disturbed' original status of the world ... must be strictly separated
from its actualisation, just as original sin is distinguished from concr
sin. In other words, the homosexual disposition must not be viewed o
the same level as concrete acts of homosexual behaviour: it is essenti
to mark off those parts of our lives which in a morally relevant sense
are more under our control (behaviour) from that which is often much
less so (disposition). Secondly, says Thielicke, 'the predisposition
itself, the homosexual potentiality as such, dare not be any more
strongly depreciated than the status of existence which we all share as
men in the disordered creation that exists since the Fall.'[11]

But while we are all part of the Fallen order, homosexuality cannot
be put on the same level with the normal created order of the sexes, b
'is rather a habitual or actual distortion or deprivation from it.'[12] It
follows from this that the homosexual condition is not to be affirmed n
idealised, but to be 'regarded as something that is questionable.'
Sherwin Bailey put it this way:

> The normal and divinely ordained human condition is the
> heterosexual, and homosexuality, strictly speaking, is an
> aberration - though not one for which the subject is
> responsible or culpable... Heterosexuality and homosex-
> uality are not alternative human conditions, nor is the invert
> (man or woman) a sort of tertium quid between male and female;
> he is an anomaly whose sexual disorientation bears its own
> tragic witness to the disordering of humanity by sin.[13]

This does not, of course, mean that a friendship between homophiles does not have any valuable aspects. It may be open to display possibilities of creativity such as are present in any close human bond. Nor should it follow that the Christian response to those of a homosexual orientation will be 'hostility, rejection or recrimination'. It is to the Church's shame that people of homosexual orientation have too often been shown hostility rather than fellowship. It is not in question that homosexual persons may have a place within the fellowship of the people of God - nor indeed that their sexuality is fully part of their whole selves seeking fulfilment. The question only concerns how homosexual sexuality may be fulfilled within the will of God. The preceding discussion does mean, however that homosexual relationships cannot, from the perspective of biblical theology and morality, be affirmed as 'natural' alternatives to heterosexual ones.

This theological perspective which sees homosexual orientation in terms of an abnormality, finds echoes in the writings of some (but by no means all - we noted a wide divergence of views in chapter 1) clinical psychologists and therapists. Replying to G. C. Davison's proposal, for example, that therapy should no longer be offered to homosexuals with a view to changing their orientation, but that therapists should instead concentrate on improving the quality of their clients' interpersonal relationships,[14] Irving Bieber writes:

> It comes down to whether homosexuality is, in fact, normal or is the consequence of and expression of psychopathology. If, as Davison thinks, homosexuality is normal, then patients who seek a change in sexual orientation should be dissuaded. If, as I think, homosexuality is pathological, the failure to develop prophylactic programs or provide therapeutic services for people who wish to become heterosexual would be a grave error...

> As to the assumption that homosexuality is normal: Over the many years of my work with many colleagues on this subject, we have found no supporting evidence, Hooker's much quoted studies notwithstanding...[15]

Bieber then outlines his own studies of which he affirms, 'in every case I have examined, studied or treated, homosexuality was the consequence of serious disturbance during childhood development. It never represented a normal segment in the spectrum of sexual organisation.'[16] His data cover non-patient as well as patient homosexuals. Bieber is critical of the prejudice against homosexuals which is prevalent in Western culture, and suggests that changes in 'irrational mass attitudes' may be brought about by presenting the public with the realities of the condition. But even so, he concludes thus:

> But promulgating a new myth that homosexuality is a normal variant of sexuality does not alter social prejudice. Few

63

believe it or can be made to believe it. And the only ones
the new mythology hurts are the homosexuals themselves.
It robs them of options and undermines the determination
needed for a reconstructive, therapeutic experience.[17]

In other words, recognising the abnormality inherent in the homosexual
orientation, does not foreclose the option of change, and of hope.

Two further points must be made. First, in the above discussion in
this chapter, 'homosexual orientation' refers to a relatively settled
sexual disposition. It does not refer to those whose developing
sexuality is passing through the generally agreed and identified phase
in normal maturation, the adolescent phase of 'incipient' homosexual
preference, which will normally develop into a heterosexual orientation.
In 'Reflections on Homosexuality' John Kleinig comments that 'because
much of human sexual behaviour is learned, the characterisation of a
person as homosexually oriented should await the establishment of a
relatively settled pattern of sexual disposition. It has been suggested',
he says, 'that the term should not be used of anyone under the age of 25.'[18]

But if that is so, it is particularly unhelpful that pressure is put on
some young people and students, some still in an adolescent phase of
development, to 'come out as gay', when without such pressure,
heterosexual development would have been likely. O'Donovan comments
on the Christian

> obligation to provide reliable and trustworthy information on
> the subject, for example to young men who may be ill-informed
> about the phenomenon of 'incipient' homosexuality that is
> common to their stage of life. No knowing the facts that would
> relieve their anxiety, they may suppose themselves incapable
> of normal sexual development, and may become susceptible in
> their despair to the unscrupulous propaganda of those who have
> no interest in spreading medical or psychological knowledge,
> but want only to recruit partisans.[19]

And secondly, we can now find some way into the question 'Can a person
choose his/her sexual orientation?' If as A. W. Steinbeck and many
others believe (cf. chapters 1 and 2) the homosexual disposition is
acquired or learned rather than innate or inborn, then in some sense
(though much less so for some than for others), it involves choice.
The decisive area of choice may have rested with the parents and
others in the early environment of the child, and the relationships
which to a great extent enable or inhibit normal sexual development.
But part of the choice may sometimes rest with the person concerned.
Often it seems the choice may be motivated mainly by unconscious
factors: a defence against some fundamental fear and anxiety, and a
reparative adaptation to strengthen damaged self-esteem and make good
defective interpersonal relationships. But if the formation of
dispositions is the result of an interaction between socialising forces

acting on us, and our own choices in response, such formation is not always beyond personal control. Dennis Altmann remarks:

'I can't help what I am' is a frequent comment in homosexual conversation. I suspect that this is less true than the orthodox wisdom suggests and that there is at least sometimes an element of deliberate choice in the adoption of homosexuality.[20]

It would certainly seem to be true of any behaviour pattern, that the more it is followed, the more fixed it becomes. In chapter 1 we also noted Don Milligan's suggestion in The Politics of Homosexuality that for some, adoption of homosexuality is a political act, in protest against the nuclear family, patriarchy, sex roles, capitalism, etc. For many, however, the element of personal choice seems negligibly small, and the pain and despair for them of 'being the victim' of a homosexual disposition is not to be minimised. While on the one hand, appeals to some sort of environmental determinism overlook the extent to which humans are 'learning animals', on the other hand, as Kleinig puts it,

Control is a matter of degree, and those who counsel reorientation or restraint too glibly have failed to appreciate the complexities of their own personalities and the subtle pressures to which they have been subject. In hypersexualised societies such as our own, psychosexual development tends to involve a precarious balancing of conflicting demands. Casually to expect people to undertake radical change in their sexual disposition is to threaten not only that balance but also them.[21]

This is not to say that counselling for change should not be sought. It is to say that no therapy (including Christian counselling) may be glib or casual. Despite the pain, it can however, be a means of support and growth. And the determination to seek help and the possibilities of living with less pain, are real options to those who do not close the door on hope of change by affirming homosexuality as 'natural'.

NOTES

[1] J. Babuscio, We Speak For Ourselves (SPCK, 1976).
[2] Op. cit., p. 5.
[3] Ibid. p. 10.
[4] Ibid. p. 5.
[5] Cf. K. J. Dover, Greek Homosexuality (Duckworth, 1978), p. 165.
[6] Testament of Benjamin 9.1.
[7] Testament of Naphtali 3.4.
[8] O. M. T. O'Donovan, 'Is It A Natural Alternative?', Insight (Wycliffe College, Toronto, June 1978), p. 6f.

[9] Ibid.

[10] H. Thielicke, The Ethics of Sex (James Clarke, ET 1964) p. 282.

[11] Ibid., p. 283.

[12] Ibid.

[13] D. S. Bailey, ed. Sexual Offenders and Social Punishment (Church Information Board for C/E Moral Welfare Council,1956). Appendix 1: 'The Homosexual and Christian Morals', p. 75f.

[14] G. C. Davison, 'Homosexuality: The Ethical Challenge', Journal of Consulting and Clinical Psychology (1976), 44/2, p. 157ff.

[15] Irving Bieber, 'A Discussion of "Homosexuality: The Ethical Challenge"', Journal of Consulting and Clinical Psychology (1976), 44/2 p. 163 ff.

[16] Ibid. p. 164.

[17] Ibid. p. 166.

[18] John Kleinig 'Reflections on Homosexuality', Australian Journal of Christian Education, Papers 59, (Sept. 1977), p. 32ff.

[19] O. M. T. O'Donovan, op. cit.

[20] D. Milligan, The Politics of Homosexuality (London, Pluto Press 1973), quoted in J. Kleinig, op. cit.

[21] J. Kleinig, op. cit.

4. WHAT ARE CHRISTIAN NORMS FOR SEXUAL BEHAVIOUR?

A. W. STEINBECK'S paper (our chapter 2) indicates that

It is impossible on the evidence from endocrinology to claim
that homosexuality is of a developmental nature, which might
obviate responsibility for behaviour pattern. . . .

The conclusion to which his paper points is that a person can choose what
to do, or not to do, with his or her sexual desires. The reality of choice
raises the question (for heterosexual as well as for homosexual): 'what
are the Christian moral norms for sexual behaviour?'. Perhaps, however,
the prior question ought to be 'are there any norms as such?', because the
antinomian approach of some contemporary literature speaks in terms of
the abandonment of a morality that is related in any way to the 'law of God'.

In his critique of Towards a Quaker View of Sex,[1] Paul Ramsey[2] argues
that a crucial choice in Christian ethics is between act-responsibility
(which seeks to determine the morality of an act only in terms of the
context of that particular act) and rule-responsibility, which acknowledges
that there are rules of action which embody Christian responsibility. The
Quaker group, discussing heterosexual intercourse, ask when it is right
for intercourse to take place.

It should not happen until the partners come to know each other
so well that the sexual contact becomes a consummation,
a deeply meaningful total expression of a friendship in which
each has accepted the other's reality and shared the other's
interests.[3]

But, says Ramsey, if that is when not, when should it? Whereas the
Quakers want to affirm that there are no fixed rules for sexual behaviour
(their historical survey, they believe, 'supports us in rejecting almost
completely the traditional approach of the organised Christian church to
morality, with its supposition that it knows precisely what is right and
what is wrong, that this distinction can be made in terms of an external
pattern of behaviour, and that the greatest good will come only through
universal adherence to that pattern ... Love cannot be confined to a
pattern ... '),[4] they do, in fact, says Ramsey, despite themselves, reach
the border where Christian love embodied in an act had to become
Christian love embodied in a general rule, or where what he calls act-
agapism, fully explored, was about to be replaced by rule-agapism.
Ramsey quotes the Quaker's essay again:

Could we say also that at least in spirit each should be committed
to the other - should be open to the other in heart and mind?
This would mean that each cared deeply about what might happen

to the other, and would do everything possible to meet the
other's needs and lessen any suffering that had to be faced.
It would mean a willingness to accept responsibility....
Should there also be a commitment to a shared view of the
nature and purpose of life?[5]

Why not, asks Ramsey, affirm all this, reminiscent as these words
are of the marriage vow? Precisely because they are. Precisely because
that would be a rule or a pattern embodying responsibility.[6] Therefore
the Friends say:

At once we are aware that this is to ask for nothing less
than the full commitment of marriage, indeed most marriages
begin with a much less adequate basis.[7]

But then they demur: 'It is worth holding in mind as a challenge both to
the quality of marriage and to that of relationships outside it; but we
cannot use it to legislate or to draw clear lines between good and evil'.[8]
They refuse, in other words, to see the law of marriage (not to be
simply identified, be it carefully noted, with the marriage ceremony) as
embodying Christian responsible action. Thus, comments Ramsey, the
question of the meaning of responsibility in sexual ethics was simply
begged in behalf of act-agapism or act-responsibility.[9] He accuses the
approach of the Quakers, which seeks to decide morality in terms only
of acts themselves and not in terms of love-embodying rules also, as
being untrue to the conclusions to which their own findings point. Not
only, he continues is 'act-responsibility' wrong (even on the Quaker's
own premises), but 'he is a poor constructive ethicist who... rules out
the possibility that rules of action may still be fashioned by hearts
instructed by Christ to know what love itself implies.'[10] Ramsey thus
rejects the 'question-begging prejudice in favour of act-agapism or
act-responsibility ethics'.[11]

Precisely the same point would count against the situation-ethics
approach of a great deal of Gay Christian literature.

In his clear and sympathetic study Time For Consent[12], for example,
Norman Pittenger guides us to the point where he affirms two criteria
for determining the goodness or sinfulness of an act:

First, there is the inner spirit with which it is performed ...
the decision to act in a fashion which will promote the
satisfaction of the subjective aim of the person in God's love
and with the widest commonalty involved in the decision.
Second, there is the intentionality which is present in the
act ... I mean by the word 'intentionality' that both parties
to the act understand the nature of what they are doing, its
real meaning, the purpose in all true love of some genuine
degree of faithfulness or loyalty, and acceptance of its
implications for both of them.[13]

Hence, he says, the question we must ask does not concern specific acts considered in isolation from their context. The real question is

Does this or that act, whatever it is, contribute in its own proper way to the movement of this person to the attainment of the subjective aim which establishes him as the man he is meant to be - always remembering ... that no person is 'discrete' either. He is always and inevitably, precisely because he is a man, a participant in the human race and in its movement towards its intended goal of a society of love and in Love.[14]

Pittenger then asks how homosexual acts fit into this pattern.

Insofar as they contribute to the movement of persons towards mutual fulfilment and fulfilment in mutuality, with all the accompanying characteristics of love, they are good acts. Insofar as they do not contribute towards mutual fulfilment in love, they are bad acts. But that statement is too brief to be exact. For in every act, however 'bad' it may be in the circumstances, there is some element of good.[15]

Clearly there are, therefore, for Pittenger, some patterns of attitude and behaviour which embody love, and some which do not. The point of difficulty, however, comes in the understanding of 'love'. When love is defined so subjectively in terms of 'inner spirit' and 'intention' it becomes impossible to guard against self-deception. The New Testament linking of the love of God with 'keeping his commandments' (1 John 5. 3), becomes obscured when God's will for us is determined by human reason or subjective spirituality alone. Whereas the Reformers, both in theology and ethics, sought to balance the subjective illumination of the Holy Spirit with an objective standard, the written Word of God, much of the situation-ethics approach of the Christian homophile movements abandons the notion of God's revealed will, or seeks to rely on a rather loosely defined concept of love, or on what it believes to be the witness of the Spirit without recourse to the Word. This leads to a morality appropriate only for 'intellectuals' - for those, in other words, who can think out carefully their motives and intentions, and who are able to assess the full extent of the appropriate 'context' in which their intentions are to be actualised - and indeed for 'intellectuals' who are ready to trust their own judgement (which fails to reckon with sin, or plain stupidity). The sort of situationism which reduces ethics to the single principle of 'love', then, all too often finds ways of bringing under that principle actions which traditional Christian morality has regarded as forbidden. For the Bible reveals a God who loves some actions and forbids others; there seems within situationism to be no space for saying that some actions are invariably bad.[16]

The heart of the difficulty with the approach of the Quaker Group to heterosexual behaviour, and of some Gay literature, notably Pittenger's study, to homosexual behaviour, is a misconstruction of the relationship between love and law in the Bible. The Biblical understanding of the nature of love is always related to the description or expression of God's character in himself on the one hand, and of the character of life appropriate for the people of God, on the other hand. Thus 'the LORD loves you and is keeping the oath which he swore to your fathers, that the LORD has brought you out with a mighty hand, and redeemed you' (Deut. 7.8), undergirds the commandment to 'love the LORD your God with all your heart and with all your soul and with all your might. And these words which I command you shall be upon your heart.' (Deut. 6.4-6). Likewise the Ten Commandments are recorded as the response required of people whom the LORD 'brought out of the land of Egypt, out of the house of bondage'. (Deut. 5.6). Similarly, the Apostle declares that 'In this is love, not that we loved God but that he loved us and sent his Son to be the expiation for our sins. Beloved, if God so loved us, we also ought to love one another.' (1 John 4.10f.)

Love is determined by the character of God. This is the central significance of the Hebrew torah (translated 'law', but originally meaning 'fatherly instruction', in this instance from God). It is the underlying basis for the relationship between love and law in the New Testament also. Jesus himself says 'He who has my commandments and keeps them, he it is who loves me.' (Jn. 14.21). The love of God is described as distinct from neighbour-love (Matt. 22.37f.), and the teaching to love God, and to love neighbour, are themselves part of the torah teaching itself (Deut. 6.4; Lev. 19.18). Further, even neighbour-love is directed by law (understood as the character of God's holy love): 'By this we know that we love the children of God when we love God and obey his commandments.' (1 Jn.5.2). Paul is perhaps clearest in the New Testament that believers are 'not under law but under grace' (Rom 6.14), by which he means precisely that a Christian's standing before God is no longer determined by law-keeping as a system of salvation, or (as it had wrongly come to be thought within Judaism)by depending on national privilege; Rom 7-8, esp 7.1-6 . But this does not mean that the law has no place in a Christian's pilgrimage towards holiness; on the contrary in Romans 13;8-10, for example, the commandments are summed up in the exhortation to neighbour love, and the appropriate pattern of behaviour for those of 'the light' is found in 'putting on the Lord Jesus Christ' and in making 'no provision for the flesh' (vv 11-14). Similarly, in terms of Christian growth in holiness (running the race) and 'doing all for the sake of the Gospel', Paul describes himself as 'under the law of Christ' (1 Cor 9.21; cf. 23-4; cf. also Gal. 6.2).

There is therefore a certain character, a certain pattern of life and response, appropriate to those who are the 'redeemed people of God', those who are 'in Christ'.

Now of course Pittenger is right that 'inner spirit' and 'intention' are part of the essence of godly behaviour. They are recognised as such in the Old Testament torah (Deut. 6.4; Lev. 19.18). They are explicitly said to be so in the New Testament, most clearly in the Sermon on the Mount

70

(Matt. 5-7), and particularly in the teaching that intentions may be as sinful as external actions (e.g. Matt. 5:28). And situation-ethics is right to the extent that it criticises an unbiblical legalism which speaks in terms of keeping a law-code as the sufficient condition of goodness before God. But it is more consonant with the entire biblical approach to the relationship between law and love, which we have sketchily outlined, to affirm with Ramsey that Christian responsibility is not a matter of the quality of individual acts only, but of their congruence with known (or knowable) love-embodying rules also.

For sexual ethics, what then are the 'commandments', the biblical principles, which embody loving behaviour pleasing to God? In terms of specific 'commandments', the seventh of the Decalogue against adultery is an affirmation of the divine will for the permanence and exclusiveness of heterosexual marriage (see discussion in chapter 5), and this is the presupposition underlying the Pentateuchal marriage laws, and the theology of marriage in the New Testament (cf. Matt. 19; Mark 10; Eph 5 etc.) In other words, the negative cast of the seventh commandment to some extent hides the positive affirmation which underlies it. And that positive affirmation of the good of created sexuality, and its appropriate genital expression within heterosexual marriage, underlies also the delight of the man for his woman in the Garden (Gen 2.23f.), and the integrating joy of sexual experience evidenced in the Song of Songs and in Proverbs 5.18f, for example.

In his book Sex For Christians, Lewis Smedes isolates three specific biblical norms which unpack more fully the divine intention for human sexuality and sexual behaviour. We shall use them as the basis for our own discussion:[17]

1. The sexuality of every person is meant to be woven into the whole character of that person and integrated into his quest for human values.

2. The sexuality of every person is meant to be an urge toward and a means of expressing a deep personal relationship with another person.

3. The sexuality of every person is meant to move him toward a heterosexual relationship of committed love.

The first norm is derived from the understanding of human sexuality as the expression of something 'God-like' in us. 'Let us make man in our own image ... male and female he created them'. (Gen 1.26-7). Smedes speaks of the biblical affirmations of life as 'body life'. The Pauline emphasis on the unity of physical and spiritual aspects of humanity in sexual relationship (in 1 Cor 6, for example) also points to this norm. This is an affirmation of sexuality. There is, however, a built-in complementarity and sexual polarity between male and female in the text of Genesis from which this norm derives, and in the New Testament discussion of sexual responsibilities in marriage in 1 Cor 7 and Eph 5.21f. This norm, let it be acknowledged, has not been central in traditional

71

Christian attitudes to sexuality, which have often leaned harder on the negative approach of Augustine than on the more positive teaching of the biblical authors. Thankfully the importance of sexuality as part of humanity is now increasingly widely affirmed within and without the Christian Church. In this context, norms 2 and 3 defining the appropriate expressions of human sexuality in loving relationships are increasingly important.

Norm 2 is perhaps most clearly illustrated in the New Testament from 1 Corinthians 6, where Paul seems to be countering the reductionist philosophy 'the body is for sex and sex is for the body, and that is all' (as we may paraphrase v. 13). On the contrary, Paul asserts that, despite all belief and appearance, for a man to join himself sexually to another (a prostitute, for example, v. 16) is to engage in an activity that was intended inseparably to join them in a life union 'For, as it is written, the two shall become one' (v. 16). The union with a prostitute is of course a caricature of the 'one flesh' of Gen 2. 24 which should be defined as the coming into being of a unitary partnership of man with wife, symbolised and deepened by sexual union. It is none the less a pointer to the fact that there is 'no such thing as casual sex, no matter how casual we may be about it.'[18] This second biblical norm for sexual behaviour is an affirmation of the inclusive meaning of sexual relationships: every part of the person is involved in a sexual union – the sexual union symbolises and deepens personal relationship at all levels. This norm is therefore broken in any sexual encounter in which the other is used as a sex-object only, and is not embraced as a person. With this much Christian homophile literature is of course in full agreement.

However, although it is right to say that sexual intercourse involves the whole person, it does not follow that to be a whole person necessarily involves sexual intercourse. This is not to deny the importance of human sexuality as a means of expressing love, nor to deny the central significance of the body as its significant vehicle. It is rather, by 'unequivocal declaration of faith in the body as the most precious instrument of communicating love' an affirmation that 'chastity, preserving sexual integrity, is a natural and desirable concomitant'.[19] Sexual activity is body-language by which personal relationship and love may be expressed. But it is not the only mode of such expression, and (as we shall discuss under norm 3) it is the appropriate mode only within heterosexual marriage, and not outside it.

In our Lord we are shown the fulness of human life. 'He knew both as God and as man, the importance of human sexuality as a means of expressing love'.[20] His own sexuality found its appropriate expression in the fulness of his being in relation with others without sexual intercourse, and he stands as a model (and present source of help) for those whose calling it is to learn to enjoy the fulness of humanity in relating as sexual persons but without genital expression.

As Jack Dominian comments in relation to the celibacy of the

(Catholic) priesthood and the single person in religious communities, 'the sustaining, healing and growth of the human person (which the married heterosexual may find in marriage) needs to go on just as much in the single person ... single people, far from denying their sexuality - whatever its intensity - accept it and make it a part of their conscious self'.[21]

The Christian Church needs to reaffirm the joy, the creative possibilities and sometimes the duty of living a celibate life. By spreading his relationships with brothers and sisters in the Christian fellowship, the Christian celibate may be enabled to enjoy the essence of fully loving and committed personal relationships but without the genital expression of them which is appropriate in marriage.

The third of Smedes' biblical norms affirms that heterosexual love is normative sexual love. Some of the reasons for this we have already discussed in chapter 3; the exegesis of Scripture which supports this will be examined in chapter 5. At this point it is valuable to recall the discussion of 'the Morality of Homosexual Acts' given in Sexual Offenders and Social Punishment', edited by D. Sherwin Bailey. In the debased and often incorrect usage of today, he says, 'sex' has acquired a predominantly physical and venereal significance, but for the theologian it retains its original, primary connotation of existence as male and female.[22] In the mutual complementarity and yet radical dissimilarity of male and female 'lie the integrative and creative potentialities of sex'.[23] Bailey continues:

> While many forms of relation between man and woman may serve to release the creative dynamic of sex, one in particular is distinguished from the rest because it involves the use of sexual organs; this, in all its varying phases and modes of expression, is the complex psycho-physical experience of coitus...
>
> The purpose of coitus may be described as conceptional and relational.... While these two purposes are to be carefully distinguished, neither must be isolated from the other. This does not mean that man and woman have not the freedom and the moral right to decide conscientiously that any concrete act of coitus shall be (so far as it lies in their power to make it) non-conceptional ... They may not, however, so separate the relational from the conceptional purpose as to exclude the latter entirely and permanently, thus rejecting the vocation to parenthood which is always implicit in union as 'one flesh'.[24]

The biblical notion of 'one flesh' holds together in an inseparable unity the life-uniting and life-creating aspects of sexual intercourse.[25] In exposition of this theme, Paul Ramsey says that the crucial question is not the order of preference to be assigned to the procreative and unitive purposes of sex and marriage; 'It is rather the question whether sexual intercourse as an act of love should ever be separated from sexual

73

intercourse as an act of procreation'.[26] His answer is not a denial of the responsibility of 'planned parenthood', but the fact that 'planned parenthood may still rest upon a religious regard for the sex act in itself both an act of love and an act of procreation'.[27] Or as Raymond Johnston puts it:

> The tension between a married pair's enjoyment of each other in the 'one flesh' relationship and the procreative possibility of each sexual act is surely rightly resolved by allowing for a distinction but not a total separation between the unitive and the generative aspects of the couple's coming together.....

Contraception can resolve this tension, and is thus, in principle not morally problematic. Indeed, in a world in which population control is necessary (in contrast to the biblical world in which population increase was desired), contraception may often be Christian responsibility. However, as Johnston continues,

> the two privileges of marriage, separable as they now are (i. e. through contraception), should never be intentionally totally separated, except for some overridingly serious and exceptional reason.[28]

Indeed, in the complete separation between the unitive and the procreative aspects of sexual intercourse increasingly common today, Paul Ramsey believes the Christian may hear 'more than faint echoes of the hoofbeats of one or another of the Four Horsemen of the Apocalypse because of the violation this is working upon the very meaning of man-womanhood in our time'.[29]

Furthermore, and to return to Bailey, the use of the sexual organs is limited by these two unique creative functions: they are the means by which the 'one flesh' union is established and deepened, and they are the means by which children are conceived. It is not accidental that the same act serves the two ends. It is clear, says Bailey, that both functions 'confine the use of the sexual organs within the bounds of an exclusive and lifelong relationship - that is to say, within the married state as the Church has always understood it.'[30]

From this it appears that the appropriate use of the sexual organs, governed by the nature of sex itself, and by these two related purposes of sexual intercourse, is reserved for the context of a personal relationship which is both heterosexual and marital.

Bailey finally turns to the claim that some homosexual acts, like those of heterosexual marriage, are 'relational', that is they are a means of expressing love. He notes first that such use of the sexual organs does make an inevitable absolute separation of the relational and procreative aspects. But he then asks what is meant by 'love'? There are, he acknowledges, homosexual relationships based upon strong and honourable

74

affection, enhanced by mutual sympathy or by mutual satisfaction in the enjoyment of a creative friendship. Such friendship may be expressed in words or acts of endearment.

This reputable homosexual 'love' may exist between men or between women ... comparable in some measure to it (though they have their distinctive qualities) are various kinds of heterosexual 'love' - for example, that of father for daughter, of sister for brother, of close friends for each other. Both types of 'love' have characteristics in common, but their special distinguishing feature may be termed chastity, or the total exclusion of venereal expression.

In contrast to them stands another 'love' which is sui generis - a love between man and woman which seeks fulfilment in the establishment of the 'one flesh' henosis, the creation of a unique common life in marriage, and the building of a family..

It will be evident ex hypothesi that such a love ... and the union in which it results, cannot possibly have any parallel in homosexual relationship. While, therefore, we may not deny that homosexual love can be a true and elevated experience, we must insist that it is one to which expression may not be given in sexual acts - a limitation which it shares with all forms of heterosexual relationship except one.[31]

We began this discussion with a statement of Smedes' three biblical norms for sexual behaviour. It now remains to be noted that all three norms belong together. The difficulty of some gay Christian argument is that it seeks to separate 1 and 2 from 3; in other words it affirms the goodness of created sexuality (1), and the unitive value of sexual intercourse (2), and then makes the improper conclusion that since certain homosexual acts can seem to fulfil both these norms, their goodness can be affirmed alongside heterosexual acts. The mistake, however, is to isolate sex as the central factor in relationship. In the biblical material, it is not sex but marriage which is used as the analogy by which God's relation with his people, Christ's with his Church is understood; and marriage is a committed, exclusive and heterosexual relationship. It is therefore norm 3 (the heterosexual relationship of committed love) which overarches and contextualises the goodness of created sexuality and the unitive value of sexual intercourse. Any sexual behaviour (whether of homosexual or heterosexual) other than exclusive heterosexual marriage falls outside this biblical norm.

Finally, therefore, we come again to the question 'Can a person choose what he/she does with his/her sexual orientation?'. The Biblical channeling of sexual intercourse within the heterosexual marriage covenant indicates that in terms of behaviour we do have a freedom of choice, for which we are therefore responsible. While Paul certainly recognises that sexual passions are strong (cf. 1 Cor 7.9 etc.), that

sexual temptations are often hard to handle, and that possibilities of
failure are therefore high, his injunctions to all to abstain from immorality (porneia: 1 Thes. 4. 3; 1 Cor 6. 18; 7. 2; Gal 5. 19 etc.) and his
teaching that even within marriage there may be times when particular
restraint is appropriate (1 Cor 7. 5), gives no support to the suggestion
that sexual inclinations must necessarily be given physical expression.
There is therefore an area of moral choice which is under our control.
The decision, for both heterosexually and homosexually inclined persons
is whether or not that choice is to be exercised within biblical norms.
In one sense, therefore, the homosexual person is in a similar situation
to the heterosexual person who would like to marry, but cannot, and who
does not feel himself or herself to have a clear calling to a life of
celibacy although a gradual realisation of the increasing liklihood of
remaining single is rather different from starting with a certainty, as
it is for some - of the impossibility of marriage. In another sense,
homosexually oriented Christians are in a similar position to others
whose early learning experiences and inherited dispositions have left
them with inclinations whose expression is incompatible with the biblical
norms of behaviour (like a hasty temper, or inhospitableness).[32] All such
people need the support of a fellowship which is sensitive to their
particular stresses, and supportive in times of strain and difficulty. At
another level, however, homosexual persons in general and homosexual
Christians seeking to live within biblical norms in particular, are in a
more difficult position than heterosexual Christians with unhelpful
dispositions. John Kleinig makes this wise comment:

> Humans are highly sexual animals and the stability of our
> personalities is fairly closely bound up with the stability of
> our sexual lives. Insofar as homosexually oriented people
> have the same levels of desire as anyone else, sexual abstin-
> ence, especially in close relationships, places them under
> considerable personal stress. Given, further, that in most
> advanced capitalist societies sex has become a commodity,
> the tensions are exacerbated. For homosexually oriented
> Christians this is made more unbearable by the fact that they
> can at present expect little but suspicion, hostility or ridicule
> from the Christian congregation should their disposition
> become known. . . .
>
> No wonder that gay churches have begun to emerge. Mis-
> guided though their theology may be, they stand as a judge-
> ment on the fellowship of believers.[33]

We shall need to take up this point in our discussion of the need for a
supportive fellowship within which homosexually inclined persons feel
they fully belong, in chapter 6. We simply note here that there are biblical norms for human sexual behaviour; norms which preclude the
genital expressions of homosexual affection; and that homosexually
inclined Christians are thus placed in a situation of particular stress, in
which a more than usually supportive fellowship is needed for them to

find appropriate fulfilment of their sexuality and an experience of the sufficiency of the grace of Christ.

NOTES

[1] A. Heron ed. Towards a Quaker View of Sex, Friends Home Service Committee (1963) (herinafter: TQVS)

[2] P. Ramsey, Deeds and Rules in Christian Ethics, SJT Occasional Papers No 11, (1965).

[3] TQVS, p. 45.

[4] TQVS, p. 39.

[5] TQVS, p. 45.

[6] Ramsey, op.cit., p. 7, cf. p. 13.

[7] TQVS, p. 45.

[8] Ibid.

[9] Ramsey op.cit., p. 7.

[10] Ibid. p. 12.

[11] Ibid. p. 13.

[12] N. Pittenger, Time For Consent (SCM 1976^3).

[13] Ibid. p. 72.

[14] Ibid. p. 73.

[15] Ibid.

[16] Cf. J. I. Packer, 'Situations and Principles', in B. N. Kaye and G. J. Wenham eds, Law, Morality and the Bible, (IVP, 1979), 151f.

[17] L. B. Smedes, Sex For Christians, (Eerdmans, 1976), p. 42.

[18] Smedes, op.cit., p. 129.

[19] J. Dominian, Cycles of Affirmation, (DLT, 1975), p. 54.

[20] Ibid.

[21] Ibid., p. 69.

[22] D. S. Bailey, ed. Sexual Offenders and Social Punishment, Church Information Board, for C/E Moral Welfare Council (1956), p. 74.

[23] Ibid.

[24] Ibid.

[25] Cf. D. J. Atkinson, To Have and To Hold, (Collins, 1979), 77-83.

[26] P. Ramsey, One Flesh (Grove, 1975), p. 8.

[27] Ibid.

[28] O. R. Johnston, Who Needs the Family? (Hodder and Stoughton, 1979), p. 83f.

[29] P. Ramsey, One Flesh, (Grove, 1975), p. 13.

[30] D. S. Bailey, op.cit., p. 75.

[31] Ibid., p. 76.

[32] Cf. J. Kleinig, 'Reflections on Homosexuality', Australian Journal of Christian Education, Papers 59, Sept 1977, p. 32ff.

[33] Ibid.

5. HAVE WE MISUNDERSTOOD THE BIBLE?

DAVID BLAMIRES is undoubtedly right when he speaks[1] of the Church's attempts to come to terms with the facts of contemporary homosexual experience being marked by the publication of D. Sherwin Bailey's book Homosexuality and the Western Christian Tradition (Longmans) in 1955. It is the first work of serious scholarship which in a deeply humane way challenges the traditional exegesis of certain biblical statements, and therefore challenges the tradition of Christian opposition to homosexual acts which has remained unbroken since the early Church. As Blamires says: 'All subsequent serious study of homosexuality from the Christian view-point either is indebted to Bailey's work or must take issue with it.' The following paragraphs fall into both those categories.

What is not in dispute is that throughout its history the Christian Church has, until very recently, expressed a united mind, severely condemning all forms of homosexual behaviour as contrary to the will of God. The latter half of Bailey's work gives a detailed account of Christian attitudes to the end of the Middle Ages with a further chapter on English Law. He argues that this tradition derives from 'the powerful influence' that the story of Sodom in particular and other biblical material more generally have had 'upon the thought and imagination of the West in matters of homosexual practice'. However, the primary thesis of Bailey's work is that this influence has been wrongly based, and needs severe criticism. His argument rests on these four points:

1. The story of Sodom is in fact not concerned with homosexual practice at all, and is irrelevant to the Christian's approach to the question of homosexuality.[2]

2. The Old Testament has two passages which specifically condemn homosexual practice, but their contexts are so different from our own that they 'give us no guidance in dealing with the manifold and complex problems of sexual inversion.'[3] We must consider the term 'inversion' in due course.

3. Four New Testament passages specifically condemn homosexual practices (three concerning males, one concerning females), but 'our knowledge of the life and social underworld of the first century enables us to set (Paul's) words in their correct context'. While they give 'decisive biblical authority' for censuring the conduct of those whom we may describe as male perverts, such as the depraved paederasts and catamites of the Satyricon, do the Apostle's strictures, asks Bailey, 'apply also the homosexual acts of the genuine invert, and in particular to those physical expressions of affection which may take place between two persons of the same sex who affirm that they are "in love"?' Bailey argues that the New Testament can hardly be said to speak to

78

such situations 'since the condition of inversion with all its special problems was quite unknown at that time.[4]'

4. Underlying much of Bailey's thesis is the distinction he maintains between the "invert" and the "pervert". Of the former, Bailey says that the Bible and Christian tradition know nothing; their strictures are directed solely against the acts of the 'pervert' who is 'not a true homosexual, but a heterosexual who engages in homosexual practices.[5]'

Each of these arguments needs to be examined carefully. We shall look at them in turn (commenting sometimes on the use to which they are put in some Gay Liberation literature), and seek to assess them in the light of a more widely framed theology of sexuality than Bailey gives.[6]

(A) Sodom and Gibeah
There are two stories in the Old Testament which have traditionally been understood to express severe divine hostility towards homosexual acts. In Genesis 19, Lot is described as offering hospitality to two angelic visitors, whose stay is interrupted by the intrusion of men of Sodom demanding 'Where are the men who came to you tonight? Bring them out to us that we may know them.' (v.5). In response, Lot begs them to desist from 'acting so wickedly' (v.7), and instead offers his daughters 'who have not known man' in the place of the visitors. It is only the angelic protection afforded by the latter which prevents an assault being made, and they warn Lot to flee the city 'because the out-cry against its people has become great before the Lord, and the Lord has sent us to destroy it.' (v.13). Soon after Lot has escap ed, the cities of Sodom and Gomorrah are destroyed by 'brimstone and fire from the Lord out of heaven' (v.24).

A similar incident is recorded in Judges 19, where 'base fellows' (v.22) from Gibeah demand that the master of a house who has offered hospitality to a wayfarer (v. 17) and his companions, should 'Bring out the man who came into your house that we may know him.' (v.22). The host replies (v. 23) 'No, my brethren, do not act so wickedly; seeing that this man has come into my house, do not do this vile thing. Behold, here are my virgin daughter and his concubine; let me bring them out now. Ravish them and do with them what seems good to you; but against this man do not do so vile a thing.' (v. 24). The incident ends with the gang rape and murder of the concubine.

Traditional Christian exegesis has understood 'that we may know them', 'acting wickedly', 'so vile a thing', as referring in these passages to homosexual assault. But it was not only homosexual assault which brought divine judgement against the men of Sodom. It was (as many older commentators, and indeed other writers in the Old Testament itself acknowledge), their proud defiance against God-given norms, and the fact that they 'proclaim war with virtue and bid open defiance to it'.[7] It was their shameless attitude which led to Isaiah's condemnation of defiant sinners as those who 'proclaim their sin like Sodom' (Isa. 3.9) and to Ezekiel's description of the sin of Sodom as including 'pride, surfeit of food, and prosperous ease, failure to aid the poor and needy' as well as the fact that they were haughty and did 'abominable things' (Ezek. 16.49).

Now Sherwin Bailey questions any reference to homosexual sin in the stories of Sodom and Gibeah. He argues that the Hebrew yadha, 'to know', although sometimes used to denote 'have coitus with', much more frequently means simply 'to know', and may only mean 'get acquainted with'. He then suggests that the demand 'to know' the visitors whom Lot entertained meant simply 'get acquainted with', and may well only have implied some serious breach of the rules of hospitality, rather than have any sexual connotation at all. He goes on to develop this theme, concluding that the 'homosexual' interpretation of the 'sin of Sodom' developed later at the hands of the Pseudepigraphists and Josephus and Philo, and so came to be accepted by the Christian Church. The interpretation by the New Testament author (Jude 7) that the men of Sodom 'acted immorally and indulged in unnatural lust' is then explained by Bailey as influenced by pseudepigraphical texts (especially Jubilees), and that RSV's 'unnatural lust' should be rendered 'gone after strange flesh' (referring to supernatural non-human beings).[8]

This interpretation of Bailey's of the Sodom incident in terms of hospitality and not homosexuality is now widely influential. (It is précis'd exactly, for example, in the GCM pamphlet The Bible and Homosexuality; and J. J. McNeill's The Church and the Homosexual, while acknowledging that 'Bailey may have overstated his case'[9] nevertheless leans heavily on Bailey's thesis).

But Bailey's interpretation is open to serious criticism, one recent commentator even noting that 'the doubt created by Dr. Bailey has travelled more widely than the reasons he produces for it. Not one of these reasons, it may be suggested, stands any serious scrutiny.'[10]

In the first place, it is very difficult to understand the weight of biblical understanding of the 'sin of Sodom' in terms only of rules of hospitality (important as they may well have been: Bailey does not give details here; indeed he cautiously notes that 'our ignorance of local circumstances and social conditions makes it impossible to do more than guess at the motives underlying the conduct of the Sodomites.)[11]

Thus the men of Sodom were 'wicked and great sinners before the Lord' (Gen 13.13), affluent (14.11); the 'outcry against Sodom and their sin is very great (18.20). Deut. 29.23 interpreted the 'overthrow' of Sodom and Gomorrah as stemming from the 'anger and wrath' of God, and of its influence as 'poison' (32.32). When rebellion against God destroys the nation, the people are described as being 'like Sodom' (Isa 1.9); and godless splendour and pride is likewise condemned (Isa 13.19). Sexual immorality of various sorts is associated with Sodom (Jer 49.18) which 'God overthrew' (50.40), in 'punishment' (Lam 4.6). 'Sodom'

became a byword for lewdness and abomination, including sexual sin
(Ezek 16.46-58),and Amos (4.11) and Zephaniah (2.9) refer to Sodom as an
example of divine judgement on pride and godlessness.

The New Testament refers to Sodom as a pointer to divine judgement
(Matt 10.15; Lk 10.12) specifically related to refusal to acknowledge
God's kingly rule. Sodom betrayed an unawareness of divine revelation,
and a careless disregard for divine concerns (Lk 17.29). It became
(2 Pe 2.6) an example to those given to ungodliness, licentiousness, the
'lust of defiling passion'; and of those who (Jude 7.8) immorally indulged
unnatural lust, defiled the flesh, and rejected authority. Sodom is used
as a symbol of apostasy in Rev. 11.8. This rather tedious list
demonstrates that while not excluding breach of hospitality the 'sin of
Sodom', was seen in general as the proud defiance of God-given norms,
with a clear sexual component. It is not possible therefore to sustain
the denial of any condemnation of homosexual assault in the total biblical
picture of Sodom's transgression.

Furthermore, it is certainly not satisfactory to decide the meaning of
yadha, 'to know', as Dr. Bailey does, by statistics (otherwise the less-
common meaning of a word would never be probable). The word does
have a very wide range of meanings, including to know, find out, perceive,
discriminate, experience, consider, be acquainted with, have sexual
intercourse with, be skilful in, be wise, etc. Indeed it is of interest that
according to the Hebrew Lexicon of Brown Driver and Briggs, which
Dr. Bailey himself quotes[12] of the 943 times yadha occurs in the Old
Testament, 17 refer to sexual intercourse, and 28 to 'get acquainted with'.
(We note in passing the carelessness with which Dr. Bailey's scholarship
is sometimes used: says Norton in The Biblical Roots of Homophobia
for example, 'The term for 'know' is used only 10 times in a sexual sense
in the O.T... and used in the sense of 'get acquainted with' 933 times.
The odds against a homosexual usage in this one instance, then, are
almost 100 to 1, and virtually every biblical scholar has now abandoned
this theory - a point challenged by the rejoinder to Norton by James
Martin)[13] Only the context can decide meaning, and as Dr. Bailey
himself notes, yadha can only refer to sexual intercourse at other
points in the same two incidents (Gen 19.8 and Judges 19.25) and it seems
difficult to deny that it should bear the same meaning three verses earlier
in each passage.

It seems more than likely, therefore, that the proud defiance of God-
given norms concerned not only those of courtesy, but those of sexual
relationship, and that the men of Sodom were bent on homosexual assault.
Likewise, while many commentators do see the primary reference of
Jude 7 to unnatural relationships between the men of Sodom and angelic
beings[14] Jude 8 is linked with Jude 7, and 'while sexual immorality in
general is clearly indicated, a specific reference to homosexual
activities can hardly be excluded.[15]'

To Bailey's further point that the historicity of the narrative cannot be taken for granted, the reply must be made that – even were there grounds for taking the text to be legendary rather than historical, it is none the less a part of the canon of scripture, and the moral judgement which it records – whatever its literary form – is no less valid.

In summary therefore, while Bailey may well be right in his rejection of the view that the story of Sodom forecloses any further discussion of the subject, and has of itself determined for all time what attitude the Church and State ought to adopt towards the problems of sexual inversion,[16] he is undoubtedly mistaken in his view that the story of Sodom has no reference to the question of homosexuality at all. While the Christian Church may well have been wrong in an over-emphasis on the significance of this one story, it does seem virtually certain that the traditional exegesis of the story of Sodom, and the support this gives to the view that this sort of homosexual assault stands, alongside all other sin, under divine condemnation, is most clearly in line with the intention of the biblical authors. It would not be valid, however, on the basis of this one story alone, to regard genuine and tender expressions of homosexual love as equally condemned.

(B) The Levitical Laws

In Leviticus 18 and 20, the Mosaic law bans among other things incest, adultery, bestiality, and homosexual behaviour. Lev 18.22 reads: 'You shall not lie with a male as with a woman; it is an abomination.' Likewise, Lev 20.13 reads: 'If a man lies with a male as with a woman, both of them have committed an abomination; they shall be put to death, their blood is upon them.'

In both verses, homosexual behaviour is described as toebah, translated 'abomination'. This is a word with wide usage in the Old Testament, but which with reference to people always denotes an offence either against a person's moral sense or against their religious integrity. Thus 'every shepherd is an abomination to the Egyptians'(Gen 46.34); so is eating with foreigners (Gen 43.32). When the abomination is 'before the Lord', toebah sometimes refers to practices derived from idolatry (e.g. 2 Ki 16.3); sometimes to sacrifices offered in the wrong spirit (e.g. Isa 1.13), or to 'lying lips' or 'divers weights' (Prov 12.22; 20.23). According to commentators, it expresses the 'idea of something loathed by God'[17] a thing which God 'detests'[18] something which is 'incompatible with the nature of Yahweh'[19] a violation of divinely ordained boundaries. The primary reference thus appears to be incompatibility with the character of Yahweh, and not merely to 'what is not proper according to Jewish law and custom", (pace McNeill)[20] In Lev 18.22 and 20.13, therefore, homosexual behaviour is thus censured as toebah: as incompatible with the nature of the Creator. K. Grayston goes even further in the suggestion that these verses provide 'an outstanding reversal of what is natural'[21]

Bailey agrees that 'it is hardly open to doubt that both the laws in Leviticus relate to ordinary homosexual acts between men, and not to

ritual or other acts performed in the name of religion'.[22] He points out
that the fact that these laws occur in chapters which expressly associate
homosexual acts and other immoralities with the customs of Canaan and
the Egyptians may suggest that the object of the legislation was to prevent
contamination of God's people by heathen depravity. However, he finds
the evidence from Egypt, Assyrian and Hittite sources very meagre, but
such as it is, 'it plainly contradicts the opinion that homosexual practices
were accepted without question'.[23] He finds it difficult to know why
Leviticus should then associate homosexual acts with the doings of the
lands of Egypt and Canaan, and suggests that this is a piece of rhetorical
denigration by an over-zealous patriot.

In his forthcoming commentary on Leviticus, however, G. J. Wenham
says that the prevalence of the customs denounced in Lev. 18 is well
attested; homosexuality is evidenced in Mesopotamia.[24]

Nonetheless Bailey concludes that the biblical text condemns homosexual practices (infrequent as they probably were) in the strongest terms.[25]

Bailey's cautious uncertainty as to the relevance of the Levitical laws
to the contemporary Christian church, and his view that they 'give no
guidance in dealing with the manifold and complex problems of sexual
inversion'[26] is more problematic. Such uncertainty (in what is undoubtedly a difficult area of biblical interpretation) is manifested also in
more recent literature, from which we isolate the increasingly influential treatment Is the Homosexual My Neighbour? by Scanzoni and
Mollenkot.[27] Commenting on the Holiness Code (Lev. 17-26) in which
these laws occur, the authors note that it includes commandments 'not
to eat meat with blood in it, not to wear garments made of two kinds of
cloth, not to plant fields with two kinds of seeds' and so on. They then
conclude from this:

> Consistency and fairness would seem to dictate that if the
> Israelite Holiness Code is to be invoked against twentieth-
> century homosexuals, it should likewise be invoked against
> such common practices as eating rare steak, wearing mixed
> fabrics, and having marital intercourse during the menstrual
> period.[28]

While they rightly point out that 'even in the most conservative Christian
circles a consistent system of interpreting Scripture is seldom applied'[29]
their proposed answer - the abandonment of the relevance of the Old
Testament - is not the only course open. The more difficult (and
essential) task is that of elucidating its relevance for contemporary
Christian faith and morality. There appear to be three aspects to this,
on which we make some comments. First, the exegesis of the text of
Old Testament ethical prescription in its own proper context, (a).
Secondly, the seeking out of underlying ethical principles in specific
Old Testament ethical prescriptions, (b). And thirdly, an examination
of the reinforcement or abrogation of the various Old Testament

prescriptions in the New Testament, and the mode of application, if any, of the underlying principles in a New Testament context, (c).

(a) Exegesis and context[30]
Leviticus 18 appears to have the form of a covenant treaty:
v. 2 Preamble: I am the Lord your God
    3 Historical retrospect: 'Egypt'
    4 Basic stipulation: 'do my laws'
    5 Blessing 'he will enjoy life'
 6-23 detailed stipulations
24-30 Curses: the consequences of transgression.

Israel's sexual morality is discussed in Lev. 18 as something that marks it off from its neighbours as the Lord's special people. Chapters 18-20 of Leviticus set out the foundation principles of a social morality for the people of God, and chapter 18 opens with a consideration of the sacred character of marriage, against which unions which are regarded as incestuous (vv. 6-18), and other Canaanite customs to be avoided (vv. 19-23), are measured as sinful. Homosexuality is referred to in v. 22, but it will be appropriate to examine the whole paragraph 19-23 in some detail.

v. 19: This verse concerns the avoidance of intercourse with a woman during 'menstrual uncleanness'. The reason for the prohibition is given in Lev. 15. 19-24, a chapter concluding the discussion of chapters 11-15 concerning the rituals designed to cleanse the tabernacle of unclean-nesses in the Israelites (16. 16). Discharges from the sexual organs (ch. 15) were sources of ceremonial uncleanness. Those who were so unclean could not participate in tabernacle worship until they had become clean again. The purpose of the regulations (including that of 15. 19, and therefore of 18. 19) is described in 15. 31 as aiding the people to know what counted as uncleanness, so that they did not 'defile the tabernacle'. To the question 'Why were these particular conditions regarded as unclean?', several answers have been given. In his commentary on Leviticus (forthcoming), G. J. Wenham quotes the view of Douglas (Purity and Danger), that holiness is symbolised by physical perfection, and that all bodily discharges were understood as defiling. But discharges were not simply incompatible with holiness, they also symbolised breaches in the nation's 'body politic'. 'The threatened boundaries of Israel's body politic would be well mirrored in their care for the integrity, unity and purity of the physical body.' In other words, the Lev. 18. 19 ruling could well have given symbolic expression to the law banning intermarriage with the Canaanites, and the prohibition against foreign custom which conflicted with Israel's status as holy nation. Furthermore, as Wenham comments, in ancient Israel factors would combine to make menstruation much rarer than monthly: early marriage, breast feeding, late weaning, and the liking for large families. 'The only women likely to be affected by Lev. 15. 19-24 would be unmarried teenage girls'.

84

v. 20: Adultery is likewise defiling, and directly contravenes the seventh commandment, which as Derrett points out[31] is a prohibition against na'af: all sexual irregularity outside the context of the 'one flesh' marriage union described in Gen 2.24. The seventh commandment thus expressed a positive definition of the will of God for the sanctity of 'one flesh' permanent heterosexual marriage.

v. 21: The law against 'spiritual whoredom', evidenced by the idolatrous practices of sacrifice to Molech, is appended to the law against physical unchastity.

v. 22: The law against homosexual behaviour must likewise be seen as an affirmation of the integrity and sanctity of 'one flesh' heterosexual marriage; its designation as 'abomination', we have already noted, refers primarily to its incompatibility with the nature of the creator who made, 'in his image', 'male and female'.

v. 23: Bestiality is likewise condemned as a heathen practice which cuts against the divine intention for sexual behaviour within the context of marriage.

vv. 24-30: These verses then outline warnings of the spiritual consequences of transgression; these individual sins defile the land and infect the whole community of Israel.

Chapter 19 then continues the exposition of social morality, with its constant refrain: 'I am the Lord' indicating that its specific precepts, in all the varied areas of social life, represent in some way an application of the character of God to the human situation.

Chapter 20 then discusses the legal sanctions to be applied in cases of transgression. Specifically, 20.13 now makes homosexual behaviour with child sacrifice, adultery and bestiality, into a capital crime.

(b) and (c) Underlying Principles and their use in New Testament
In his book The Authority of the Old Testament, John Bright makes the point in his discussion of the laws concerning transfer of property in Lev. 25, that although the law itself is now irrelevant to our situation, the entire chapter (25) is undergirded by, and expressive of, a very definite theological concern.[32] It is the task of the Christian interpreter to 'detect behind every biblical text... that facet of theology which expresses itself there'.[33] In other words, the Christian task in approaching Old Testament moral prescriptions (and specifically here in Lev. 18.6-23) is to ask what is the theology which undergirds it, and how can that theology be made 'actual' in our context. The application of principle may be identical in our day as in the Levitical context (Bestiality is prohibited); the application may be different (as e.g. where the regulations for ceremonial uncleanness have been abrogated and 'spiritualised', along with the sacrificial system). With reference to Lev. 18. 6-23, two primary principles seem to be operative. First: the
85

requirement for the separation from other nations and their idolatrous practices (cf. 18.1-5; 20.1-7), and with that, respect for the rules of cleanness for tabernacle worship. Secondly, the regulating of sexual behaviour in the light of the commandment against na'af which upheld the 'one flesh' pattern channelling full sexual expression into monogamous heterosexual marriage.

Much of the detail of application of the first principle was rendered obsolete by the redefinition of the people of God in supra-national terms, while the appropriateness of the laws defining ritual uncleanness was lost with the abrogation of the sacrificial system by the death of Christ. The requirement for moral holiness remained however, and found continued expression in personal and church terms in the New Testament ethical teaching (cf. Gal 5:16f, Eph 4:1f, Phil 2:14f, Col 3.5f, 1 Pe 1.14f etc.). The principle of monogamous heterosexual marriage is also upheld in the New Testament references to 'one flesh' (Matt 19.5; Mk 10.8; 1 Cor 6.16; Eph 5.31).

It is further to be noted that the death penalty is prescribed for homosexual offence. This penalty (which, as with all criminal sanction, appears to have been a maximum penalty, without certainty as to its enforcement)[34] was prescribed for a range of crimes: premeditated murder, man-stealing, persistent disobedience to authorites and parents, adultery, homosexual offences, the worst forms of incest, false prophecy, profanation of the sabbath, blasphemy, idolatry, magic and divination.[35] Apart from incest and homosexuality, every other capital offence can be directly related to a law of the Decalogue. It would seem more than probable, therefore, that a primary factor in the seriousness with which incest and homosexual behaviour was viewed, was their contravention of the principle of the seventh commandment which upheld the sanctity of marriage.

Despite the plea of Scanzoni and Mollenkott and others, there seems no way of avoiding the conclusion that the Levitical prohibition against homosexual behaviour is a specific - if negative - restatement of a fundamental divine principle for sexual relationships, namely that physical sexual intercourse belongs within monogamous heterosexual 'one-flesh' marriage. It is that theological principle which is the basis for the view that all homosexual behaviour falls outside the will of God for human sexuality.

(C) St. Paul
Apart from brief references to Sodom in 2 Peter and Jude (in contexts referring to sexual sin), the only New Testament writer to make specific reference to homosexuality is Paul.

In Romans 1.18ff, he is teaching that God's wrath (his personal, though never malicious or in a bad sense emotional, reaction against sin)[36] is revealed against all ungodliness (asebia) and wickedness (adikia) of men, who by their wickedness suppress the truth. From the creation of the world, the eternal power and very Godhead of God have been clearly perceived, and the cause of the revelation of God's wrath is that, although men knew God sufficiently to know what they ought to be and do, they did not glorify him as God (v. 21), but rather gave way to idolatry (vv. 22-23). Barrett comments: 'The process by which idolatry becomes moral evil is neither automatic nor impersonal: God handed them over, as punishment, by the lusts of their own hearts, to an unclean life.[37]

Paul's first example of the way men dishonour God and so as a result dishonour their own bodies (v. 24) he describes in this way:

> For this reason God gave them up to dishonourable passions (pathe atimias.) Their women exhanged natural relations for unnatural (para physin) and the men likewise (homoios) gave up natural relations with women and were consumed with passion for one another, men committing shameless acts with men and receiving in their own persons the due penalty for their errors. (1. 26-7).

A number of comments are necessary. First, the context is set by reference to 'ungodliness' and 'wickedness'. Anders Nygren[38]does not see any great distinction in meaning between these two words in this context. 'We come closest to Paul's thought if we regard the two words as simply an emphatic expression of one and the same thing. A wrong relationship with God and the wrong behaviour linked with it are together set in contrast to the 'righteousness of God' of which Paul has just spoken in 1. 17. The full significance of adikia anthropon in this context is found in its contrast to the diakosune theou. In other words the 'unrighteousness' of the Gentiles described in the following verses (not only of sexual relations but the whole list of adikia of v. 29ff), is understood as contrary to the character of God, whose 'righteousness' is revealed in the Gospel. (vv. 16-17). This context is further clarified by noting that part, at least, of the background to Paul's thought here is the doctrine of Creation. (v. 20: 'ever since the creation of the world'). In Gen 1. 27 and Gen 2. 7, 21f., humanity is described as created by God as male and female. The creation pattern for human sexuality is heterosexual, and the marriage covenant (implicit in Gen 2. 24, and explicit elsewhere in Scripture) centring in 'one flesh', is the background for Paul's understanding of human sexual relationships, (just as much as it is the basis for the Levitical laws, of which, of course, Paul was well aware).

When Paul then speaks of pathe atimias, shameful passions of a sexual nature, (cf. 1 Thes 4. 5, Col. 3. 5;), which are given expression in 'unnatural' (para physin) relations, 'unnatural' must clearly then mean 'unnatural' in terms of God's heterosexual pattern in creation. On this basis, all homosexual behaviour together with all distortions in heterosexual sexuality, is 'unnatural', and by reference back to adikia (v. 18), is consequently in some way contrary to the character of the 'righteous' God.

87

It is not therefore sufficient to regard Paul's condemnation as covering only the homosexual behaviour of those involved in idolatrous paganism, as some writers have suggested. On this view, homosexual behaviour between Christian believers who were not worshippers of pagan idols is thought to be exempt from Paul's censure. But Paul does not argue that the homosexuality of any given individual is related to that person's faith or idolatry. It is rather, as Lovelace puts it[39]'a product of the damaged social fabric in a society of idolaters.' The disorders of Romans 1.24-32 are not wrong because they issue from specific idolatry, but wrong in themselves (as contrary to the character of the Creator), and Paul refers to them as evidence of the spiritual bankruptcy of idolatrous cultures[40]. It is noteworthy also that Paul's reference here is to man as man, and is not only concerned with the discipline of the Christian fellowship.

It has also been argued (notably by McNeill[41]), that para physin (contrary to nature), which describes the relationships between women (v. 26), though the men are 'likewise'(v. 27) included in the same judgement, is sufficiently ambiguous to allow for the excepting of some forms of loving homosexual behaviour from Paul's otherwise universal censure. McNeill comments on the different way physis is used in Paul's thought (Rom 4.18 concerning the grafting of a wild olive - the Gentiles - onto a cultivated olive tree - the Jews; 1 Cor 11.14: 'Does not nature teach you that if a man has long hair it is a shame unto him'; and other references in Gal 2.15; 4.8; Rom 2.27; Rom 2.14). McNeill suggests that, with the exception of Gal 4.8, 'the character referred to by physis does not necessarily represent something innate, but could be a matter of training and social conditioning'[42] He goes on to suggest that there is a parallel between para physin and the Old Testament concept of toebah, which McNeill understands to mean 'not according to Jewish law and custom'[43](we have argued for the inadequacy of that understanding of toebah earlier). McNeile therefore considers that para physin in Rom 1.26 may refer either to the individual (heterosexual) pagan who goes beyond his own sexual appetites in order to indulge in new sexual pleasures, or to those who fail to conform to what he calls the Jewish-approved customs of the Levitical laws.

Now even if McNeill is right, this would still mean that Paul is understanding homosexual practices to be examples of behaviour characteristic of heathen ('not natural to the people of God'). In other words, Paul is expressing a moral judgement against such practices, and placing an obligation on his Christian readers not to indulge in them. Paul was selective concerning which customs of contemporary society were consonant with the freedom of the Gospel (such as the legitimacy of eating food offered to idols in some circumstances 1 Cor 8.1f), and which were not. He is clear, even on McNeill's reasoning that homosexual practices are among the latter. And furthermore, he is careful to refer not only to Gentiles: he is referring to sexual misconduct among all men, whether Jew or Gentile, by his inclusion of the Jews in the 'very same things' (Rom 2.1, 17-24).

88

However, such an interpretation as McNeill's does not allow
sufficiently for the varied usage of physis in contemporary Greek,
which makes the determination of meaning from context the more
important. The Dictionary of New Testament Theology comments that
physis is a typically Greek (as opposed to Hebraic) concept, used among
the Stoics of 'nature' as distinct from the concepts of culture, custom or
morality. In Philo, physis is often used for the work of God in creation.
It refers to the regularities of the order of nature, to the natural
condition of things (like elements), and often denotes the nature of man.
In Josephus, the word is used of innate dispositions, natural qualities,
and the regular order of nature. Paul's usage sometimes parallels
that of Philo and Josephus ('Jews by birth' in Gal 2.15, means 'descent,
extraction'). Sometimes it has more in common with Stoic usage in
indicating what Jews and Gentiles have in common - the regular order
of nature which determines the distinction between the sexes.[44] Allowing
the context of Romans 1 to decide usage would indicate that para physin
here means 'contrary to the order of creation' i.e. 'contrary to God's
creation pattern', rather than McNeill's more restricted interpretation
in terms of Gentile anti-Jewish customs, or merely pagan perversity.

To the further suggestion that para physin in Rom 1.26 can refer to
'doing what comes naturally' (thereby exempting the homosexual
behaviour of exclusive homosexuals from Paul's censure), the reply
must be made that Paul's understanding of the whole of the 'natural'
order is that it is now disordered and disturbed (cf. Rom 8.20-22).
Rather, as Lovelace comments:

> All human sexuality, in its heterosexual as well as its homosexual
> forms is disordered by the inherited drive toward disobedience
> which we call original sin, and by the broken social fabric
> of idolatrous societies. Human sin and God's punishment
> upon it have deeply affected the processes by which sexual
> identity is formed, with the result that none of us, hetero-
> sexual or homosexual, naturally desires to fulfil perfectly
> God's plan for our sexuality. We did not consciously choose
> to have the deviant sexual orientation which drives us toward
> fornication, adultery or homosexual practice. But we are
> confronted with the choice whether or not to act out our orien-
> tation and fulfil our natural desires, or whether instead to
> seek the control and transforming power of the Spirit of Christ
> to restrain and reorient our desires and our behaviour.[45]

To be sure, the responsible caring gentle sexual behaviour of Christian
homosexuals expressing tender affection for each other is hard to recognise in Paul's tone in Romans 1. However, while 'doing what feels right'
can, as Lovelace says, be exhilarating, it can also be deceptive.[46] The
point at issue, however, is that moral guidance comes not in terms of
'what feels so right cannot be wrong', but rather in terms of which
sexual acts are in conformity with God's revealed will. No Christian
moralist has ever proposed that what 'feels' right or natural should

be the sole or sufficient criterion of goodness or holiness in Christian living.

In addition to the Greek background to Paul's thinking in Romans 1, W. D. Davies[47] also discerns in these verses evidence of dependence on the Rabbinic conception of Gentile behaviour, expressed in the so-called Noachian commandments. These were reckoned as laws binding upon every living soul, given to men in their nature before the special revelation to Israel on Sinai. One of these 'commandments' was the prohibition of adultery, which (as we have discussed earlier) was a negative statement of the principle of exclusive heterosexual marriage. Paul would certainly have shared the view that the Levitical prohibitions expressed the will of God concerning homosexual practice. In other words, from both Greek and Hebraic strands in Paul's thinking, we derive the conclusion that Paul's own position agreed with that of the Levitical texts, and the creation principles underlying them, that all homosexual practices were a departure from the will of God for human sexuality.

We do need to stress at this point that Paul is plainly referring to homosexual behaviour, not to temptations, or dispositions (although we should probably include within 'behaviour' the 'intention to behave' in a certain way, implied in Paul's reference to 'shameless passions' (1.26)). His concentration of behaviour is evident from the descriptions of the passages concerned, and to his subsequent comment in Rom 2.2 that 'the judgement of God rightly falls on those who do such things.' He includes within his list, of 'all manner of wickedness' covetousness, malice, envy, murder, strife, deceit, malignity, gossiping, slander, haters of God, insolent, haughty, boastful, inventors of evil, disobedient to parents, foolish, faithless, heartless, ruthless. In other words, in the light of the revealed character of the Creator, homosexual behaviour along with any other of these attitudes and actions is in Paul's judgement perverse and under divine wrath. Paul is clearly reacting to the prevalence of all kinds of perversity in the Gentile world of his day, and it is noteworthy that some of the other sins in his list receive comparatively little censure in the modern world. However, as we have seen, he includes Jew and Gentile together in his condemnation, and he chooses first to discuss homosexual behaviour because it suited his purpose very clearly to demonstrate the spiritual bankruptcy of a culture which had lost touch with the worship of the Creator, and its results in the reversal of what is 'natural' to God's creation pattern.

There are two other references from the pen of Paul. In 1 Cor 6.9-11 Paul asks

> Do you not know that the unrighteous will not inherit the kingdom of God? Do not be deceived; neither the immoral, nor idolaters, nor adulterers, nor malakoi nor arsenokoitai, nor thieves, nor the greedy, nor drunkards, nor revilers, nor robbers will inherit the kingdom of God. And such were some of you. But

90

you were washed, you were sanctified, you were justified
in the name of the Lord Jesus Christ and in the Spirit of our God.

The sort of behaviour mentioned here finds no place in the 'kingdom of
God' - that is the condition in which the kingly rule of God is acknowledged.[48] Paul seems clearly to affirm that the person who, without
repentance and without intention to "lead the new life following the
commandments of God", striving together with the Spirit of God,
continues a course of behaviour such as is characterised in these verses,
that person has never really become part of the 'kingdom'. As Lovelace
points out[49], biblical morality draws an important distinction between
'repentant believers prone to certain sins, but striving against their
inner and outward expression (see 1 Jn 1.6-10), and unrepentant persons
following a steady and unresisted course of planned disobedience (see
1 Jn 2.4; 3.6-9)'. Paul's point becomes trivial if it is understood only to
say that all of us are sinful. While that is of course profoundly true,
and indeed all of us are guilty of perhaps most of the sins mentioned, he
is not here simply saying 'we are all sinners'. He is rather saying that
a settled and unresisted habit of sins such as these is evidence of the
'unrighteousness' which has no place in the kingdom of God.

But who are the malakoi and the arsenokoitai? The RSV has been
guilty of distortion by translating both these two words together 'homosexuals'. The text is not referring to those of homosexual inclination,
or temptation. The majority of exegetes understand the words to refer
to 'the passive and active partners respectively in male homosexual
relations'[50]. Their meaning has been challenged, however, notably again
by McNeill. He follows John Boswell's suggestion that malakoi
(literally meaning 'soft') refers to the self-indulgent, and that
arsenokoitai are homosexual prostitutes. Neither word therefore, he
argues, necessarily refers to homosexuals in committed love relationships. However, again McNeill's exegesis borders on special pleading.
He finds support for the suggestion that arsenokoitai may refer to
homosexual prostitutes from the fact that the word is plural in form,
and the plural koitai occurs in Romans 13.13 referring to excess in
sexual behaviour. However arsen invariably means male in contradistinction to female (cf. Septuagint of Gen 1.27; 5.2; 6.19; 7.2; 9.15
etc; cf. also Matt. 19.4; Mark 10.6; Luke 2.23; Gal 3.28; and Rom
1.27 'men... with men') and koite in the Septuagint frequently connotes
the marriage bed, or sexual relationships, and in its four uses in the
New Testament, three (Rom 9.10, Rom 13.13, Heb 13.4) refer to
sexual intercourse and one (Luke 11.7) merely means bed as a place of
rest. Arsenokoitai literally therefore means a male bed-partner for a
male in sexual intercourse. The fact that malakoi are mentioned between
two other sexual sins suggests strongly that their 'softness' is not
merely 'self-indulgence' generally but, as the Arndt-Gingrich Lexicon
suggests 'men and boys who allow themselves to be misused homosexually.'

Finally in 1 Timothy 1.8-11, as part of an attack on Judaistic
legalism, Paul nonetheless affirms the restraining and normative

function of the law of God. These verses are certainly dependent on, if not an exposition of, the Decalogue, and arsenokoitai are listed with murderers, manslayers, immoral persons, kidnappers, liars, perjurers, as 'lawless and disobedient' who stand under the condemnation of God's law. After the reference to murderers and manslayers (parallel to the sixth Commandment), and before the kidnappers (David Field notes the parallel with the eighth commandment: there was a thriving black market in kidnapped slaves at Ephesus[5]) and the liars and perjurers (ninth), come the references to immoral persons and arsenokoitai. Both these, heterosexual and homosexual, are in Paul's mind linked with the commandment against adultery, in that both engage in sexual intercourse outside the one flesh marriage covenant which the seventh commandment upholds. Again most clearly, Paul's strong words apply to homosexual behaviour. The issue of disposition, or temptation, is not here being considered.

Thus far in terms of exegesis Sherwin Bailey appears to agree with our conclusions. He says that 'the technical words malakoi and arsenokoitai ... denote respectively those males who engage passively or actively in homosexual acts.[52] and he believes that Rom 1.26-7 speaks of Paul's censure on homosexual behaviour. However, he then makes a very influential suggestion, followed by McNeill and many other recent writers, based on his distinction between the pervert (heterosexuals who engage in homosexual acts) and the invert (the person of a fixed or settled homosexual disposition whom he calls the 'true' homosexual). Bailey believes that Paul's strong words apply only to the former 'such as the depraved paederasts and catamites of the Satyricon'. But the Bible does not speak, says Bailey, to those physical expressions of affection which may take place between two persons of the same sex who affirm that they are 'in love'.[53] This distinction has now become common currency in the literature of the Christian Homophile movement.

Others have suggested that Paul's ethical injunctions on sexual matters are (like head-covering for women during worship in Corinth), a matter only of cultural conditioning.[54] As with our discussion of the Old Testament moral injunctions, we need to ask what principle underlies Paul's teaching, and the answer here is clearer: In Romans, as we have noted already, Paul is specifically contextualising his discussion within the doctrine of Creation; and in 1 Timothy he is discussing behaviour patterns which in his judgement contravene the moral principles of the Ten Commandments (which themselves reflect the character of God). The question of cultural conditioning - particularly bearing in mind Paul's selectivity in his attitude to his contemporary culture - cannot be invoked to diminish the relevance of Paul's words.

But Bailey's point is a much stronger one than only cultural conditioning; it rests on the assumption that the homosexual condition was unknown in the ancient world, and that all homosexual behaviour was therefore understood as perversion of heterosexual disposition. Much of his thesis in fact rests on this assumption. But that assumption itself needs to be scrutinised.

(D) 'Invert' and 'Pervert'

There are three major factors which make Bailey's assumption of the inapplicability of Paul's comments to those whom he calls 'inverts', less than satisfactory.

In the first place, if, as is widely asserted, homosexual behaviour has characterised all societies throughout history, and if as we now know, the homosexual disposition is more or less exclusive for a minority of human beings, it seems prima facie unlikely that earlier cultures were unaware of the fact that some people had an exclusively homosexual preference.

Furthermore, as we have seen, the attitudes of Paul's day were influenced not only by the Old Testament heritage, but also by the Greco-Roman culture around them, and it would seem that within the Greek world, knowledge of an exclusively homosexual orientation (as one extreme of a spectrum of dispositions) was probable. Thus in Greek Homosexuality, K. J. Dover refers to the Athenian court proceedings of 346 BC involving a certain Misgolas. He describes Misgolas as 'a distinguished citizen but a man of "extraordinary enthusiasm" for this activity' (homosexual relations), who took Timarkhos home to live with him.[55] The quotation comes from the testimony composed by Askhines for use in court for Misgolas. This would seem to indicate a very fixed disposition. Then there is the evidence of Agathon, 'an exceptionally good looking man who in his earlier years had been the paidika (the junior partner in a homosexual relationship) of Parsanias, and continued in this relationship well into adult life.[56] - almost certainly an indication of some sort of settled homosexual partnership.

Likewise Philo refers to those who 'habituate themselves' to the practice of homosexual acts,[57] so also Josephus indicates that homosexual behaviour had become a fixed habit for some.[58] Clement of Alexandria (3rd century) refers to the interpretation of Basilides on Jesus' word in Matt. 19.12 concerning those 'eunuchs who have been so from birth', that

Some men, from birth, have a natural aversion to a woman; and indeed those who are naturally so constituted do well not to marry.[59]

It is likely therefore that Paul and his readers were not unaware of the fact that there were some people for whom homosexual intercourse was not simply a freely chosen alternative but a fixed preference or settled lifestyle.

Secondly, the Kinsey reports proposed a rating scale of 0-6 from heterosexual persons with no homosexual inclinations through to exclusively homosexually orientated persons. Since then, clinical opinion has generally accepted that there is a continum of sexual preference, and to speak of sexual preferences in terms of two absolutely distinct categories (corresponding to those whom Paul censures and those whom it is said he does not), is to oversimplify the issues. With David Blamires[60] we agree that

> the concept of the 'true homosexual' is highly problematic. The Kinsey Report makes it clear that there is a continuum of sexual orientation from 100 per cent heterosexuality to 100 per cent homosexuality. Where, from the angle of moral judgement is the line to be drawn between the 'true homosexual' and the rest?

Blamires rightly asks how the morality of a sexual act can be judged on the basis of a position on a continuum. He then, however, says that morality is concerned with the total moral, personal and social context, with relationships and responsibilities rather than with specific isolated acts[61]. We have suggested (chapter 4) that in Christian morality the moral, personal and social context for relationships and responsibilities should not be set over against the rightness or wrongness of specific acts. The Bible reveals a God to whom some acts are wrong whatever context they occur in, though the different context may affect the degree of culpability associated with such acts. We have further suggested that sexual acts (whether homosexual or heterosexual) which occur outside the hetero-sexual marriage covenant, come in that category. While, therefore the opposition of 'situationism' to 'Christian principle' may provide a way of avoiding the apparently universal biblical censure of homosexual behaviour (though we disagree with this approach) we agree that no moral distinctions can be drawn on the basis of a continuum of preferences. The existence of such a continuum makes a moral judgement based only on the categories of 'invert' and 'pervert' inadequate.

Thirdly, the New Testament concentration on behaviour undercuts Bailey's distinction in any case. By returning to the pattern of creation as the norm for human sexuality, Paul is placing all homosexual behaviour (together with all heterosexual deviations also) in the category of 'abnormality' in the moral, not merely statistical sense. It is homosexual behaviour, not the homosexual disposition, which is so strongly censured alongside other sins in the New Testament. As David Field comments on the New Testament view that homosexual conduct is wrong: 'A loving motive - vastly important though it is - cannot reverse that judgement'[62].

Within the terms of their own concerns with criminal law, the authors of the Wolfenden Report also found it important to avoid the distinction:

> Some writers on the subject and some of our witnesses have drawn a distinction between the 'invert' and the 'pervert'. We have not found this distinction very useful. It suggests that it is possible to distinguish between two men who commit the same offence, the one as the result of his constitution, the other from a perverse and deliberate choice, with the further

94

suggestion that the former is in some sense less culpable
than the latter. To make this distinction as a matter of
definition seems to prejudge a very difficult question.[63]

This is not, of course, to deny that for those whose sexual preferences
are more or less exclusively homosexual, homosexual behaviour for
them feels perfectly natural. And for them, as for heterosexual people
without prospect of marriage, the Christian behaviour pattern which
restricts sexual intercourse to within heterosexual marriage, will feel
at times to be unbearably severe. However as D. S. Bailey himself
commented in another publication:[64]

Sympathy with the homosexual's predicament cannot alter
the fact that his practices, though congruent with his condition,
are objectively unnatural and cannot reasonably be regarded
otherwise.

We must conclude from the biblical perspective, therefore, that for a
Christian homophile seeking to live within a biblical moral pattern, the
fulfilment of his or her sexuality will need to be realised in the light of
the impermissibility of expressing his or her sexual inclinations in a
physical (that is, genital) way. This raises questions both for the Christian homophile, and also for the wider Christian community - and to these
we turn in chapter 6.

NOTES

[1] D. Blamires, Towards a Theology of Gay Liberation, (SCM, 1977)
p. 9.
[2] D. Sherwin Bailey, Homosexuality and the Western Christian
Tradition, (Longmans, 1955), pp. 155-6.
[3] Ibid., p. 156.
[4] Ibid., p. 157.
[5] Ibid., p. ix.
[6] i. e. in this book; his other works include The Mystery of Love and
Marriage (SCM 1952), The Man-Woman Relation in Christian Thought
(SCM 1959); he edited Sexual Offenders and Social Punishment (Church
Information Board for C/E Moral Welfare Council, 1956).
[7] Matthew Henry's Commentary on Genesis.
[8] D. S. Bailey, op. cit., p. 16.
[9] J. J. McNeill, S. J., The Church and the Homosexual (DLT, 1977),
p. 47. Bailey's careful scholarship is also referred to, if somewhat
misused, in Rictor Norton's essay 'The Biblical Roots of Homophobia' in
Towards a Theology of Gay Liberation, Bailey is also quoted by C. R.
Austin in 'Bisexuality and the problem of its social acceptance' in Journal
of Medical Ethics (Sept. 1978), 4/3, p. 132f; and by many other authors.
[10] D. Kidner, Genesis (Tyndale Press, 1967), p. 137.

[11] Bailey, Homosexuality and the Western Christian Tradition, p. 3.
[12] Ibid., p. 2n.
[13] Towards a Theology of Gay Liberation chapters 4-6.
[14] J. N. D. Kelly, The Epistles of Peter and Jude (A. & C. Black, 1969) p. 258.
[15] Ibid., p. 261.
[16] Bailey, op.cit., p. 28.
[17] S. R. Driver in Hastings Dictionary of the Bible, art. 'Abomination'
[18] D. Kidner, Proverbs (Tyndale Press 1964) p. 98.
[19] C. H. Toy, ICC on Proverbs (1899), p. 80.
[20] McNeill, op.cit., p. 55.
[21] K. Grayston, art. 'Abomination' in A. Richardson ed A Theological Word Book of the Bible (SCM, 1957).
[22] Bailey, op.cit., p. 30.
[23] Ibid. p. 36.
[24] Wenham refers to Reallexicon der Assyriologie, 4, 459ff.
[25] Bailey, op.cit., p. 37.
[26] Ibid., p. 156.
[27] Letha Scanzoni and Virginia Ramey Mollenkott, Is The Homosexual My Neighbour? (SCM 1978).
[28] Ibid., p. 61.
[29] Ibid., p. 113.
[30] In much of this discussion I am indebted to the forthcoming commentary on Leviticus by G. J. Wenham.
[31] J. D. M. Derrett, Law in the New Testament, (DLT 1970), p. 371.
[32] J. Bright, The Authority of the Old Testament (SCM 1967), p. 153.
[33] Ibid., p. 143.
[34] B. N. Kaye and G. J. Wenham, eds. Law, Morality and the Bible, (IVP, 1978), p. 42ff.
[35] Ibid., p. 42.
[36] C. K. Barrett, The Epistle to the Romans (A. & C. Black, 1957) p. 33.
[37] Ibid., p. 38.
[38] A. Nygren, Commentary on Romans, (ET 9th printing, Fortress Press, 1967), p. 100f.
[39] R. Lovelace Homosexuality and the Church, (Fleming H. Revell Co. Old Tappan, N. J., 1978), p. 93.
[40] Ibid., p. 94.
[41] McNeill, op.cit., 54f.
[42] Ibid., p. 54.
[43] Ibid., p. 55.
[44] C. Brown ed. Dictionary of New Testament Theology (Paternoster) Vol 2, (1976), p. 660.
[45] Lovelace, op.cit., p. 94.
[46] Ibid., p. 95.
[47] W. D. Davies, Paul and Rabbinic Judaism (SPCK, 1970^3), p. 114f.
[48] e.g. G. E. Ladd, Jesus and the Kingdom (SPCK 1966).
[49] Lovelace, op.cit., p. 96.
[50] C. K. Barrett, A Commentary on the First Epistle to the Corinthians, (A. & C. Black, 1971^2), p. 140.
[51] D. Field, The Homosexual Way - A Christian Option? (Grove, 1976), p. 1

[52] Bailey, op.cit., p. 38.
[53] Ibid., p. 157.
[54] e.g. J. Orr 'Christians take another look at Homosexuality' in Australian Journal of Christian Education, Sept. 1977, referring to T. D. Perry and C. L. Lucas 'The Lord is My Shepherd and he knows I'm Gay' (1973), and other books.
[55] K. J. Dover, Greek Homosexuality (Duckworth, 1978), p. 22.
[56] Ibid., p. 144.
[57] De Specialibus Legibus 3.37-42, cf. also De Vita Contemplativa 59-63.
[58] cf. Against Apion 2.273-275 cf. other references cited by R. T. Beckwith in Appendix to this chapter.
[59] Miscellanies 3.1.
[60] Towards a Theology of Gay Liberation, p. 14.
[61] Ibid., my italics.
[62] D. Field, op. cit., p. 19.
[63] The Wolfenden Report, para. 35.
[64] D.S. Bailey, ed., Sexual Offenders and Social Punishment, p. 76.

APPENDIX
THE ATTITUDE TO HOMOSEXUAL PRACTICES IN THE JEWISH BACKGROUND TO THE NEW TESTAMENT
(a comment on D. Sherwin Bailey's Homosexuality and the Western Tradition) by R. T. Beckwith

SHERWIN BAILEY pays a good deal of attention, albeit selectively, to intertestamental and rabbinical literature. He rightly notes the unmitigated hostility of the rabbinical literature to homosexual practices (pp. 61-63). For the rest, he confines himself to ancient interpretations of the sin of Sodom, treating the traditional homosexual interpretation of this as late and mistaken (chapter 1); and to Wisdom 14.26, where he again contests the normal interpretation (pp. 45-48). In the case of Wisdom 14.26, he thinks that the reference could equally well be to transvestism or self-mutilation, but as these practices were and are often connected with homosexuality, and as they too meet with the disapproval of the Old Testament, it is questionable whether the author of Wisdom would have been as concerned to distinguish between them as Bailey is. More likely, he intended to condemn all three, and this being so, it is more probable (pace Bailey, p. 10) that a homosexual interpretation of the sin of Sodom is implicit in Wisdom 10.8; 19.14 (not 19.8, as Bailey says).

Bailey's interpretation of these latter passages from Wisdom is characteristic of his treatment of other inexplicit references to Sodom, such as Ezekiel 16.49f., Ecclus 16.8 and 3 Macc. 2.5 (pp. 9f., 21). The 'pride' or 'arrogance' of Sodom, to which Ezekiel, Ecclesiasticus and 3 Maccabees refer, was shown primarily in their refusal to heed Lot's warning of impending judgement. But why was judgement impending? According to Wisdom it was for inhospitality to strangers, i.e. to the angels (they 'received not the strangers'). This, however, is an obvious case of understatement: it was not just that the men of Sodom did not receive the strangers, but that they tried to do violence to them. And the reason for such understatement is doubtless modesty. There are some matters, as Paul says, which it is shameful even to speak of (Eph 5. 3, 12). This is an attitude which the present climate of opinion makes it difficult for us fully to understand, but the frequency with which the word 'shame' and its cognates occur in the Old Testament shows that it had a very long history among the Jews. The Jews could be explicit about such matters when they had to be, but they preferred to be reticent about them.

Bailey's refusal to see homosexual overtones in the above references to Sodom is defensible, even if mistaken, since the passages are not explicit, but his unwillingness to see such overtones in Jubilees 16. 5f; 20. 5f; Testament of Levi 14. 6; Testament of Naphtali 3. 4f; Testament of Benjamin 9. 1; Epistle of Jude 6f; 2 Peter 2. 6-8 (pp. 11-20) is not defensible. Each of these passages accuses the men of Sodom of fornication, lasciviousness, changing the order of nature or going after strange flesh. Now, it is only on the homosexual interpretation of the story of Sodom that the writers in question could have known the sin of the men of Sodom to be sexual or unnatural in this way. Bailey's idea that the passages condemn the men of Sodom not for lusting after other men but for lusting after angels is absurd, since the men of Sodom were unaware that they were angels. The only reason why the passages some-times draw a comparison between the sin of Sodom and the consorting of angels with women in the years before the Flood is that both unions were unnatural. (In all other respects the unions were dissimilar, for in the case of Sodom it was the men, not the women, that were involved, and it was they, not the angels, who took the initiative.)

It follows from this that the homosexual interpretation of the sin of Sodom can be traced back at least to the second century B. C., when the book of Jubilees was written. If, however, it is implicit in Ezekiel, it can be traced back to the sixth century B. C., and it remains the most natural interpretation of the account given by Genesis itself, at an earlier date still. This makes it unlikely that the homosexual interpretation of the story of Sodom was a reaction against Hellenistic homosexual practices, as Bailey supposes (pp. 20f., 26f.). What is much more probable is that the homosexual practices of Hellenism caused Jewish writers to state more bluntly how the story of Sodom had always, in fact, been understood.

Bailey freely concedes that Philo and Josephus present the (homo) sexual interpretation of the sin of Sodom (pp. 21-23), as they undoubtedly do, but says that such an interpretation is uncommon in the rabbinical literature (pp. 23-25). In this he is certainly mistaken: see, for example, Jerusalem Sanhedrin 10. 3; Genesis Rabbah 26. 5; 50. 5, 7; Leviticus Rabbah 23. 9; Numbers Rabbah 20. 22; Aboth de-Rabbi Nathan 12. 6; Targum of Pseudo-Jonathan, at Gen 19. 5. The rabbis do indeed go on to attribute other sins to Sodom as well, but they are in no doubt about this particular sin, which (as already mentioned) they also condemn most heartily in other contexts than the story of Sodom. So, too, do Philo and Josephus. It is not only in the context of the story of Sodom that they deal with the matter (Philo, De Abrahamo 133-141; Quaestiones et Solutiones in Genesin 4. 31, 37; Josephus, Antiquities 1. 11. 1, 3 or 1. 194f., 200f). Josephus deals with it also in Against Apion 2. 24, or 2. 199; 2. 37, or 2. 273-75, where he says that such practices are contrary both to nature and to the Law of Moses. Philo deals with it also in De Specialibus Legibus 3. 37-42; De Vita Contemplativa 59-63; Hypothetica 7. 1, where he says the same as Josephus, though at greater length. This definite and reiterated teaching in Jewish literature of the first century and in rabbinical tradition illustrates and confirms the meaning of the relevant New Testament passages in a significant way.

CHAPTERS 3 - 5 have been concerned with the challenge that the teaching of Christian homophile movements poses to the wider Christian fellowship. In chapter 3 we did not find ourselves able, from a biblical perspective, to endorse the claim that the homosexual orientation is 'natural' from the point of view of the Christian doctrine of creation. From that point of view, the existence of a continuum of sexual preferences (we are talking not about the rich variety of 'masculinity' and 'femininity' as general character traits, but of sexual orientations) is one evidence of the 'Fallenness' of our human sexuality. Expressions of heterosexuality, to be sure, have elements of 'Fallenness' (such as selfishness and lust), but the expression of heterosexual preference is in the direction of the divine pattern of what is 'natural'. The expression of homosexual preferences however, (likewise sometimes a vehicle for selfishness and lust, as well sometimes as for feelings of love), would be in a direction away from this creation pattern. In chapter 4, we were unable therefore to endorse the claim that homosexual behaviour is in every way on a par with heterosexual. On the contrary (chapter 5), the more traditional exegesis of Scripture which proscribes homosexual acts was seen, on examination, to be sound.

The fourth prong of the Christian homophile challenge, however, comes at the level of fellowship, and is probably the most crucial. Frequently homosexually oriented Christians, where their dispositions are known, have received suspicion at best, and sometimes open hostility, ridicule or worse from Christian congregations. Many therefore feel forced to keep their sexual preferences secret for fear of misunderstanding or recrimination. 'No wonder', says J. Kleinig, 'that gay churches have begun to emerge. Misguided though their theology may be, they stand as a judgement on the fellowship of believers.'

We will seek in this present chapter to sketch - all too briefly - some biblical guidelines on understanding the practice of the Christian life, applicable to all Christians whatever their particular needs; alongside this we will seek to articulate the implications of the biblical perspective of chapters 3 - 5 for the personal morality of the Christian homophile and for the health of the fellowship to which he or she belongs. But first some distinctions.

1. Personhood and Homosexuality
At the end of his 'Dialogue with the Homophile Movement'[2] Charles Curran suggests that many proponents of Gay Liberation are making the same mistake today which many churchmen made in the past (and which many still do), namely that of identifying the person with is or her homosexuality[3] Curran comments: 'a sound anthropology argues against any such identification. One can still love and respect the person, even

100

though one believes his homosexual behaviour falls short of the full meaning of human sexuality[4].' Indeed, as our earlier discussion indicated,[5] the classification of persons into 'homosexual' and 'heterosexual' obscures the existence of the continuum of sexual disposition from exclusively homosexually inclined persons to those of exclusively heterosexual orientation. Further, as Kleinig comments, to speak of a person as 'a homosexual' suggests that there is 'a diagnosable condition', whereas the 'linking feature - sexual attraction to members of the same sex - ... is not restricted to certain personality types, nor generated by a unified set of causes[6].' While, therefore, it is tremendously important to distinguish a homosexual orientation from certain sexual deviations with which it is often unfortunately associated in the uninformed mind e.g. transsexualism (although it seems that some self-labelled 'homosexuals' may be 'transsexuals'[7].) transvestism, hermaphroditism, narcissism, paedophilia (people of all shades of sexual disposition may be liable to such deviations), it is equally important not to make a dismissive labelling classification ('he is a homosexual'), which may then be magnified into an equation of sexual inclination with the whole of his person. As A. C. Kinsey and his co-workers themselves commented in relation to the behavioural dimension,

> It would encourage clearer thinking on these matters if persons were not characterised as heterosexual or homosexual, but as individuals who have had certain amounts of heterosexual experience and certain amounts of homosexual experience[8].'

The distinction between the noun ('he or she is a homosexual', which categorises 'him or 'her') and the descriptive adjective ('he or she has homosexual inclinations') must be made. The noun feeds the notion of an absolutely fixed and static view of human nature (on a par with 'he is a neurotic'), and encourages an equation of homosexual inclination with the whole of a person. The adjective ('he has homosexual inclinations', just as one might say of another, 'he has neurotic tendencies in such and such respects') both allows for an affirmation of the person without necessarily affirming the person's homosexuality, and allows for the possibilities of change and growth[9].

In their significant book Is the Homosexual My Neighbour? which we have earlier criticised for its handling of the biblical material, the authors L. Scanzoni and V. R. Mollenkott rightly give a strong Yes! to their title question, and urge the Christian church to move from what has come to be called 'homophobia' (a sense of revulsion and fear against homosexual tendencies), to understanding; to move from prejudice to the affirmation of homosexual persons as persons.[10] While we cannot agree with these authors' in their support for the validity of covenantal homosexual relationships as parallel to heterosexual marriage, we do join them in stressing the need for the Christian church to move from all appearance of 'rejection and recrimination' to an acceptance of each homosexually oriented individual person as displaying like all men something of the image of God, yet like all men subject to a sinful nature and to certain particular temptations to sin.

Two further comments are now appropriate. First, it is possible, of course, to affirm the category 'person' in a very impersonal (even condescending) way. I want to be treated as ME, the individual I am, not just as one member of the category 'person'! This need, however, should be safeguarded by an understanding of each person as 'made in the image of God' - an understanding which holds together the rich variety, freedom and creativity of personal individuality within the moral personal framework which reflects (albeit distortedly) the character of the Creator.

'You come of the Lord Adam and the Lady Eve', Aslan answered, 'And that is both honour enough to erect the head of the poorest beggar, and shame enough to bow the shoulders of the greatest emperor in earth.'[11]

Secondly, an affirmation of 'personhood' must not be pressed in a way that denies the essentially 'binary' nature of humanity (as we outlined in chapter 3). As E. L. Mascall puts it:

We have come to look upon sex in far too superficial a way, as if there were a kind of undifferentiated human nature common to all beings male and female alike, but itself essentially sexless, and that sex was imposed upon this as a sort of extra... Humanity is, so to speak, essentially binary; it exists only in the two modes of masculinity and femininity, and we can only understand it by understanding them. It does not exist partly in one and partly in the other but under a difference of mode it is fully in each.[12]

These comments draw together our responses to the two basic precepts of the Gay Liberation campaign. We recall (from chapter 1), that these are (i) that homosexuals are fully the equal of heterosexuals, and (ii) that homosexuality is fully the equal of heterosexuality. Clause (ii) is a bid for the recognition of homosexual behaviour as in every way on a par with heterosexual behaviour, a bid which we believe cannot be sustained within the biblical moral perspective as we have expounded it. But (i) is about personhood, and while the doctrine of the Fall requires us to understand the homosexual orientation as something questionable (though not usually blameworthy), and homosexual behaviour as sinful, yet the biblical view of man enables us to distinguish personhood in the image of God from its distortion and marrings through original or actual sin. In other words, we may - and must - value, love and affirm each person, while not affirming (let alone idealising) certain questionable - indeed sometimes perhaps tragic-aspects of a person's disposition, nor the overt sinful behaviour by which he or she may wish to express it.

The homosexual is my neighbour. The homosexual minority and the heterosexual majority in the Christian fellowship both need to work at the question as to how neighbour love is appropriately to be shown by each to the other.

2. Practical Christianity – a sketch of some important themes

(a) The Place of Law in the Gospel of Love
The Christian Gospel holds together the two biblical themes of law and grace. 'Law' in the biblical sense is best understood as a description of the holy character of God, and a prescription of the pattern of life appropriate for human persons made in his image.[13] 'Grace' includes the gracious gifts both of a right relationship with God in Christ and also of the inner strength of the Holy Spirit by which the holy character of God may increasingly be formed in the Christian believer (the 'law written on the heart'), and by which the appropriate pattern of life for a human person made in God's image may increasingly be enjoyed.[14] Both the gift of a righteous relationship, and the growth of a holy character are possible because of the atoning death of Jesus Christ 'in whom we have redemption, the forgiveness of our sins', and because of his resurrection, 'the immeasurable greatness of the power' of which is 'in us who believe'.[15]

The Reformers used to speak of the 'threefold use' of the law of God as part of the Gospel of grace,[16] a theme taken up more recently by A. R. Vidler in his book Christ's Strange Work.[17] In the first place, says Vidler (commenting on 1 Tim 1.8-11, in which Paul lists those who engage in homosexual acts alongside other sinners), God's law is ordained for the preservation of human society in order and justice. The Pauline passage shows that this is not only an Old Testament idea, nor is it Paul's private opinion; it is part of 'the glorious Gospel' (v.11) which was committed to him.

> God has ordained laws and authorities to administer them in order that human society, man's common life, may be preserved, and prevented from breaking up into chaos or anarchy.[18]

It is this part of the Gospel, says Vidler, which obliges Christians to take politics and social legislation seriously. Secondly, under the chapter heading 'God's law as a summons to repentance', Vidler says that God by his law summons all men to repentance, partly by setting before us a code of duty, which all in fact transgress, and partly by showing us the law's fulfilment in the Messiah, 'as something much more damning than a code of duty'.[19] This second use of the law

> rivets upon us the conviction that we cannot be justified by anything we can do. Like the Israelites in Egypt, we are commanded to make bricks without straw – to be perfectly holy when we have none of the makings of holiness – to love God with all our hearts and the neighbour as ourselves when we are without divine charity.[20]

He goes on to say that both repentance and faith are gifts from God.
Together they constitute the response which he enables us to make to
His Acts of Deliverance. Repentance is the gift which enables us to
turn round and abandon attempts at self-justification; by faith we are
enabled personally to put our whole trust in the Messiah, and the righteousness and grace of which he is the Author.[21] God, in other words, uses
his law in this second way as a summons to repentance, as part of his
gracious invitation drawing us to Christ.

In the third place, Vidler speaks of the Law of God as 'Guidance for
the Church'. This is what Calvin called its 'proper use'.[22] Vidler quotes
from the Lutheran Formula of Concord which speaks of 'the fruits of the
Spirit' being those 'works which the Spirit of God dwelling in believers
effects through regenerate men... And in this way do the children of God
live in the Law and fashion their life according to the rule of the divine
Law, which way of living St Paul is wont to call... the Law of Christ'. In
other words, says Vidler,

> It is the third office of God's Law to declare what the fruits of
> the Spirit are, which are the evidence of justifying faith. God's
> Law shows the regenerate the path that they should walk in and
> warns them whenever they are straying from it.
> The preaching of the Gospel, therefore, ought always to be
> followed as well as preceded by the teaching of the Law.[23]

Unfashionable as this emphasis on the Law of God as part of the Gospel
may be in contemporary Christian thinking,[24] it is not novel; it simply
restates and reaffirms the teaching of the New Testament, and is echoed
through the teaching of the Fathers as well as the Reformers. Vidler's
own summary is pertinent:

> The Church must speak plainly about the Law, distinguish
> between its various uses, and explain its place in God's scheme
> of salvation; but it must do this not with a view to spinning a
> pretty or impressive theory, but with a view to our living under
> a more practical and strict obedience to the Law of God - first,
> by taking our political responsibilities seriously as our duty to
> God, rather than as our ideals for humanity; secondly, by
> hearing and proclaiming God's summons to repentance; and
> thirdly, by seeing that our new life as Christians and as a
> Christian community is one in which God's Law is our standard
> and guide, while Christ's righteousness alone is our justification.[25]

In terms of our specific discussion of the questions raised by homosexuality, we shall need to clarify the ingredients of Christian fellowship
which enable each member to hear and respond to God's summons to
repentance, according to his own need, and to live out the new life
'following the commandments of God and walking from henceforth in his
holy ways.' With respect to the homosexual person, the question of
law is raised only with reference to homosexual acts. We have seen how

the Biblical attitude to homosexual acts is determined by one primary theological consideration focussed in two ways. First, homosexual acts are toebah (translated 'abomination') because they represent a reversal of what is sexually 'natural' in terms of the character of the Creator; and second, they are a contravention of the principle of the 'one flesh' heterosexual marriage relationship, which underlies both the Levitical laws and the ethical exhortations of the New Testament. On these grounds, the Bible as we have seen forbids homosexual acts. (While the Old Testament primarily has homosexual anal intercourse in mind, our discussion of biblical norms for sexual behaviour indicated that any overt sexual activity between members of the same sex related to deliberate sexual arousal is likewise proscribed.[26] The Bible is not here talking about friendship relationships between the same or opposite sexes.)

Here, then, is a moral boundary by which a Christian seeking to make a biblically informed moral judgement will approach the political, personal and ecclesiastical aspects of homosexual behaviour (though the first is mostly beyond the scope of this essay). It is a restatement in negative terms of the positive biblical affirmation of the norm of heterosexual marriage. As an Appendix to Sexual Offenders and Social Punishment (edited by Sherwin Bailey) reads:

> While...we may not deny that homosexual love can be a true
> and elevated experience, we must insist that it is one to which
> expression may not be given in sexual acts - a limitation
> which it shares with all forms of heterosexual relationship
> except one.[27]

(b) Holiness and Sin
The biblical proscription of homosexual behaviour as contrary to the will of God places the homosexually inclined Christian under particular constraints which are sometimes very stressful. But that stress is often needlessly exacerbated by confusion in a person's mind between two notions which are separated in New Testament thought: sin and temptation. Neither word features very prominently in much contemporary Christian literature, and hardly at all in the writings of the homophile movements. And yet, together with other major themes of 'repentance', 'forgiveness' and 'sanctification', they are central in the New Testament presentation of the Christian Gospel, and in its teaching about the practice of living the Christian life. We must explore their meanings more fully and relate them to the particular needs of the homosexual and the Christian fellowship of which he is part.

A proper understanding of the biblical teaching on sin begins with the biblical understanding of the nature of God, described as Spirit, as Light, as Love, and as a Consuming Fire.[28] Older theologies used to speak of God's Sovereignty,[29] his Goodness in love,[30] in grace,[31] in mercy, patience and justice,[32] and of his Holiness[33]. The last points to his majestic purity in his own Person, which is then revealed in his moral law. Jesus called the Father 'Holy Father' (Jn 17.11); and the moral injunctions of the Covenant codes of the Old Testament 'Be holy as I am holy' (cf. Lev 19.2), are taken as the text for the moral exhortation of the New Testament: 'As obedient children, do not be conformed to the passions of your former ignorance, but as he who called you is holy, be holy yourselves in all your conduct.' (1 Pe 1.14-15)

As Richard Lovelace comments in his discussion of 'The Church's Ministry to Homosexuals'

Pastors and laymen who are counselling homosexuals and homophobes must determine whether their hearers conceive of God as the holy and sovereign Lord of Creation presented in both the Old and New Testaments, or whether instead they are trying to invent a relationship with a fictitious god of some kind, an idol made of pure benevolence who is designed never to cut across their attitudes and actions with a challenge towards change and holiness. They will find that many church members today are in fact uneasy about the God described in Scripture and have exchanged Him either for an impersonal principle which does not make demands or the projected image of an indulgent parent.[34]

A recovery of the biblical vision of God in his majestic holiness, such as overwhelmed Isaiah in the temple (Isa 6.1f), will be linked with a realisation of sin as unholiness in relation to God's nature, and disobedience in relation to his moral law. The biblical doctrine of the Fall is an analysis of the fact that this state of sin is shared by every individual who has been naturally born (i.e. every member of the race except our Lord himself); human nature is now inherently sinful. As a result, sin is expressed in overt acts of sins. The Gospel records our Lord's words: 'Out of the heart come evil thoughts, murder, adultery, fornication, theft, false witness, slander'. (Matt. 15.19). The second 'use' of the law of God, which we understood as a description of his holy character, 'summons us to repentance', as Vidler put it, and, as with the Greek 'paedagogos' who acted as warder and tutor in restraining the wayward youth (Gal. 4.24), the law of God 'convicts us of being unable to justify ourselves, and thereby summons us to repentance and hands us over to the divine supernatural Liberator, who justifies us freely by his grace.' (Vidler).[35]

For the homosexually oriented person, this means a confrontation with the law of God which prohibits active homosexual behaviour. For the Christian guilty of homophobia on the other hand it requires 'an insight penetrating below the surface of legalistic and pharisaical righteousness and revealing his inner state of fear and hostility towards other sinners'.[36] As Lovelace puts it again:

Homophobes tend to define sin as the transgression of God's commands and ignore the roots of sin in alienation from God

106

and hostility or indifference to other persons. Homosexuals on the other hand err on the other side by defining sin entirely in terms of the violation of 'loving' inner attitudes which are very subjectively defined and ignore the biblical definition of love as obedience to God's commands. The gay Christian must recognise that God has not left us without objective information about the ways in which we should love him and other human beings. The homophobe must realise that love is what is commanded, and that inner dispositions which negate it must be put to death.[37]

(c) A 'new nature' in Christ

The heart of the New Testament Gospel is summed up by St Paul in the words:

> But now the righteousness of God has been manifested apart from law, although the law and the prophets bear witness to it, the righteousness of God through faith in Jesus Christ for all who believe. For there is no distinction, since all have sinned and fall short of the glory of God, they are justified by his grace as a gift, through the redemption which is in Christ Jesus. (Rom. 3.21f.)

Or again:

> When the goodness and loving kindness of God our Saviour appeared, he saved us, not because of deeds done by us in righteousness, but in virtue of his own mercy, by the washing of regeneration and renewal in the Holy Spirit, which he poured out upon us richly through Jesus Christ our Saviour, so that we might be justified by his grace and become heirs in hope of eternal life. (Titus 3.4ff).

The gift of a new 'nature' in Christ, variously described as sonship as being 'alive to God in Christ Jesus' as a 'new creation' and as 'adoption'[38] matches the nature of 'original sin' inherited from 'Adam' (Rom 5. 12-20), and includes the gift of a right relationship with God as Father (Rom 5.11), and the forgiveness of our sins through the cross of Christ (Col 2. 13-14). The Christian, united by faith to Christ, the Righteous One, is described as being free from God's wrath (Rom 5.9), free from bondage to sin's downward drag (Rom 6.6-7), free from the condemnation of God's holy law (Rom 7.6, 12; 8.1), and free from 'the law of sin and death' (Rom 8.2). These freedoms all come 'through Jesus Christ our Lord' (cf. Rom 5.21; 6.23; 7.25; 8.39); the Christian is therefore free to learn to live a new life of obedience rooted in repentance and faith, (Rom 12.1-2; 13.8-14) by 'putting on the Lord Jesus Christ' (Rom 13.14), and by walking by the Spirit and bearing his fruit. (Gal 5.16f).

The goal of the Christian life is restoration to the image of God[39], in which our human calling is to serve God with our whole being: to love him, to enjoy his fellowship, to reflect his character in the living out of the 'new nature' which is ours in Christ, in love to God and to our neighbour.[40] The gift of renewal in Christ for the homosexual Christian can mean that he is not trapped in a static bondage to an unchosen and unchangeable condition. By virtue of his 'new nature' his homosexual inclination, though usually remaining, need no longer rule his life, and he can learn to affirm and accept himself as a person affirmed and accepted by God, without affirming or expressing his homosexual desires. For the heterosexual Christian guilty of homophobia, a 'new nature' means that he need not be trapped in an unavoidable revulsion and fear towards other people whose sexual preference he cannot understand; but he can be enabled in Christ to learn how to let genuine love cast out fear, and he can learn from Christ how to give accepting and affirming love to his homosexually inclined brother or sister. The important word in these paragraphs is 'learn', for long-standing habits of mind and behaviour, especially in an area which touches our humanity as deeply as does our sexuality, are not usually quickly changed. The learning to live out the 'new nature' is a process which the older theologies called 'sanctification'. In this area of life, Christian counselling help may well be needed in discovering how to apply Christian understanding and spiritual resources to practical living.

(d) Sanctification

To use the word 'learn' with reference to the Christian life emphasises the fact that the Bible speaks of Christian living as a process of growth.[41] Sanctification - being made holy - is a process specifically linked in the New Testament with the work of the Holy Spirit in the Christian believer. 'Sanctification' holds together both God's provision ('your life in Christ Jesus, whom God made... our sanctification', 1 Cor 1.30), and our human experience of it. On this human side, the practical aspects of growing characters 'conformed to Christ in holiness', take account of the fact that the 'old nature' still - this side of heaven - exercises a downward drag of sin, but that, 'in Christ', the Christian is enabled to 'yield his members to God as instruments of righteousness.' (Rom 6) and grow in his resistance to indwelling sin. This involves both an affirmation of the goodness of 'body-life', and the consecration of every part of the personality to God. And this is a learning process. In Tit 2.12, Paul speaks of the indwelling Christ working out in us by his Holy Spirit a copy of his righteous character. In Ephesians 4, the process is described as 'putting off the old and putting on the new' (vv. 22, 24); in Gal 2.20, the Christian is described as 'crucified with Christ' and, with him, 'alive from the dead.'

This is not to say that the Christian does not sin any more. Both Scripture and experience contradict such a statement. It is to say, however, that 'the source of power and victory over sin resides in the resurrection life of Christ, mediated to the Christian by the Holy Spirit'[42] and that 'through the force of the law of the Spirit, sin is no longer inevitable, and the Christian has no legitimate excuse for the habitual practice of sin. He should not make allowance for it, but if he should fall, there is a Helper to plead his cause. [43] And that 'power' and that Helper are relevant to areas of sexual sin, to homosexual and heterosexual, as to every other area of human life. [44] It is the task of Christian counselling-care for Christian believers by each other (and particularly pastoral counselling from pastors and trained counsellors to members of congregations), to make available to Christian consciousness and experience these and other resources of the spiritual life in ways which are both spiritually responsible and therapeutically effective.

A process of Christian counselling, over a period of time, for the homosexually oriented person typically includes a focus on self-acceptance, which derives from God's acceptance of him as a beloved child in Christ, a focus on the sinfulness of homosexual acts, and the need for repentance and change from any such behaviour, and a focus on the reality of forgiveness and on progression through healing and change to thinking and living in response to God's love. [45] The order of focus in the counselling process depends - as in all counselling - on the particular needs at different times of the persons concerned, and their ability to receive counsel. Most behaviour patterns for which people seek counselling help are difficult to change because the people concerned both want to change and do not want to change. This is precisely what the New Testament leads us to expect in its exposition of the Christian life for every believer as a battle in which the personality is the field of conflict between the 'old' and 'new' natures. [46] For homosexual behaviour patterns, which contain a strong pleasurable element, the resistance to change is often high, and expert counselling help over periods of time may be required. However, Christian counselling, equipped with the message that a person is not cut off from the love of God because he perceives himself to lack worthiness, that in Christ there is acceptance, forgiveness and promise of renewing grace, can - and is - an aid to many in the pathway required for their particular sanctification.

However, transformation of behaviour patterns - whether of homosexual acts, of homophobic rejection, or any other - are not only possible; they are part of the meaning of Christian faith. Both the practising homosexual and the 'reviler' are included in the list of those of whom Paul said: 'And such were some of you. But you were washed, you were sanctified, you were justified in the name of the Lord Jesus Christ and in the Spirit of our God.' (1 Cor 6.11).

And in this process, at some stage, the Law of God as a summons to repentance will be an indispensable element. Richard Lovelace's comments are again to the point:

For the homophobe, this means a careful survey of Jesus' differing responses to Pharisees and to sexual sinners, and an examination of Paul's treatment of the internal dimensions of sin and righteousness. For those who are homosexuals, it means review of the passages in the Old and New Testament

109

which deal with homosexual behaviour, and an honest recognition
that the exegetical attempts to evade the direct meaning of these
are strained, speculative and implausible... Active gay believers
today have convinced their consciences that the Bible does not
speak negatively about their lifestyle or that if it does, it does
not really express God's will for their lives. Until this deception
is broken through by the Holy Spirit and the biblical text, there
can be no repentance and change.[47]

(e) Christian Healing
All of the above which concerns homosexually oriented Christians is
written with a view to enabling them to understand more fully the
spiritual resources which are available in Christ within the Christian
fellowship, and to affirm that it is possible to learn to be free from being
overwhelmed by their inclinations, and from the need to give their
inclinations physical expression. It has not been presumed that spiritual
maturity, with or without counselling help, will necessarily reverse the
homosexual orientation itself. However, just as reversal is sometimes
possible through therapy of various sorts, so it is sometimes the result
of growth in grace, often aided by Christian counselling and prayer for
healing.

To the extent that homosexual preference is (as Steinbeck's paper
suggests, see chapter 2) an expression of a sexual adaptation resulting from
an impaired gender identity or from fear of heterosexual relationship or
is a reparative defence to strengthen damaged self-esteem, or to counter-
act deep-seated lonliness or felt rejection, to that extent the homosexual
preference represents a psychological wounding of the personality, often
derived from early learning experiences.

There has recently been a renewed interest in, and exploration of, the
healing power of the Gospel of Christ to bring substantial healing to such
psychological wounds - described variously as 'inner healing' or 'the
healing of memories'.[48] Without necessarily endorsing any particular
'technique', we can see this as an important rediscovery of the application
of the Gospel of redemption and recreation through Christian counsel and
prayer, often reinforced by a sacramental context. One aspect of the
New Testament faith is that the work of Isaiah's Servant, who has 'borne
our griefs and carried our sorrows' (Isa 53.4), is seen in the healing
ministry of Jesus (Matt 8.17), and hence the New Testament exhortation
to 'Cast all your anxieties on him, for he cares for you.' (1 Pe 5.7)
The healing of past wounds, the enhancement of personal awareness,
the growth in positive self-acceptance are essential ingredients of love in
personal relationships[49] and the love of the Christian fellowship can be
the context in which these ingredients are received from Christ through
one another, and enabled to grow. This is not the place for a fuller
treatment of Christian healing, except to underline the fact that the Gospel
of Christ includes the possibility of substantial though not complete healing,
in time, of our emotional lives[50] and to refer to the records of Christian
testimony[51]of those whose homosexual desires have been redirected through

such means. Such persons often possess exceptional sensitivity and
special sympathy with others isolated or neglected for various different
reasons, and thus often themselves prove to be particularly effective
counsellors as they themselves grow in Christian maturity within the
fellowship.

(f) Temptation
'Lead us not into temptation', our Lord taught us to pray. In this
petition, we follow the prayer for forgiveness of our sins by asking our
Father in heaven not to allow us, his people, to come into that kind of
temptation which would lead us to fall away, but rather to rescue us
from the power of the evil one. The praying of that prayer is necessarily coupled with an acceptance of personal responsibility to avoid
situations in which such temptation is likely. However, though God
does sometimes allow his people to be tested that their faith may be
purified and their character refined (1 Pe 1.6f), and even allows
'the tempter' (Matt. 4.3, 1 Thes 3.5) a certain reign in this process
of trial, 'God is faithful', says Paul, 'and he will not let you be tempted
beyond your strength, but with the temptation will also provide the way
of escape, that you may be able to endure it.' (1 Cor 10.13).

The primary point to draw from this for our purpose is that
inducements to sin are not themselves sinful. Christ himself was
'tempted', yet remained sinless (Heb 4.15) 'Temptation becomes sin
only when and as the suggestion of evil is accepted and yielded to.'[52]

The homosexual Christian,· therefore, while needing to recognise that
deliberate intentions to act can be as sinful as acts themselves (so we
are taught in the Sermon on the Mount, Matt. 5.28), needs also to be
able to relax in the knowledge that though his homosexual inclinations
manifest an abnormality, and may make him particularly vulnerable to
temptations to translate his desires into intentions or actions, such
temptation is not itself sin. This is particularly important when, as
often seems to be the case, homosexual inclinations are a largely
unconscious defence against deep-seated fears. And the homosexual
person needs to know that the resources of God's grace to restrain
abnormal desires are available to him within the Christian community.
His, though is the responsibility to receive this grace. He can learn
how to 'submit to God... resist the devil' (Jas 4.7), and how to realise
in experience that perfect love can cast out fear.

And for the heterosexual, this important distinction between sin and
temptation obliges him to see his homosexually inclined Christian
brother or sister not as the agent, ipso facto of some self-chosen perversion, but as a creature of God like himself, forgiven and accepted
through the grace of God like himself, and one who, like himself, is
subject to temptations in particular ways, which sometimes are
particularly difficult to resist.

After expounding what he calls 'the primary dynamics of Christian
111

renewal' ('justification: you are accepted; sanctification: you are free from bondage to sin; the indwelling Spirit: you are not alone; victory in spiritual conflict: you have authority')[53] Lovelace adds this:

An informed faith is necessary to draw upon these resources of grace, and since so many Christians are ignorant of their existence, the majority of church people today are living at what the hymn writer called a 'poor dying rate'. It is not surprising that unrestrained homosexuality and homophobia are both present in the church.[54]

May God enable the whole Christian church to rediscover in experience the rich, sanctifying and healing resources of his grace.

3. Concerning the Christian Homophile
We are now in a position to attempt to draw together the implications of the biblical Gospel and of biblical morality for the Christian homophile.

(a) Personal responsibilities
We need first to reaffirm what a wide variety of human experiences and personal and emotional factors are covered by the common use of terms like 'homophile' and 'homosexual'. As Lewis Smedes has wisely commented: 'Let it be said... that no matter how sure some heterosexual people are in their moral judgements, they make them in a fog of ignorance about the deeper goings on in a homosexual's life.'[55] We are talking about persons who are made in the divine image, and who are as different from one another as are heterosexual people. We are talking almost invariably (though not quite) about people who have not chosen their condition, and who therefore are not blameworthy for it. But the homophile, like the heterosexual also, has responsibilities before God towards his own life. To quote Smedes again:

His life is a gift of grace just as mine is, and he is a steward of his life as I am. What ought he to do with his homosexuality? This too must be asked with enormous compassion. For the obstacles on his route to a moral and happy life are incalculably greater than mine. But painfully vast as his problems are, he is still a person living before God with freedom to choose, within the limits set for him by nature, what he will do with his abnormal sexuality.[56]

Smedes then outlines what he calls three steps in a responsible confrontation with one's own homosexuality: (i) self-knowledge; (ii) hope; (iii) accommodation.

Under (i), Smedes urges the homosexual courageously to face the abnormality of his condition, but at the same time to refuse to accept a burden of guilt for it. He may need help in working to 'overcome the self-doubt and self-hatred that lie beneath' his condition, but he is 'God's creature and child of irreducible worth and inestimable potential.' He must however, accept responsibility for what he does with his homosexual drives.

Under the second heading (ii), 'hope', Smedes urges the homosexual to believe that change is possible and ought to be sought. Though statistics of full conversion to heterosexuality are not promising, there are, as we have said, too many testimonies to God's help towards some degree of change for them to be discounted. Even if conversion to full heterosexuality is not possible, 'given the abnormality of the homosexual condition, a person whose tragic misfortune it is to suffer it, is morally responsible to gear his choices in the direction of changing the condition that victimises his life.[57]'

But thirdly (iii) Smedes acknowledges that some people are so deeply conditioned towards homosexual responses that change does not appear possible. For such people he says the primary moral option is celibacy, a choice which should be weighed with the utmost seriousness. At this point it is important for us to make brief comment on our understanding of the Christian vocation to celibacy appropriate for heterosexual as well as homosexual people. Both marriage and celibacy are described by Paul as 'special gifts' from God (1 Cor 7.7). Paul further demonstrates that there are circumstances (such as he believed to be true of Corinth in view of the expected 'impending distress', 7.20) in which singleness may properly be chosen in preference to marriage for the sake of 'undivided devotion to the Lord' (7.35). Matthew's Gospel also records Jesus' reference to those to whom celibacy is 'given', namely 'those born impotent, those made impotent by physical means, and those who have voluntarily renounced marriage in order to devote all their time and energies to the service of the Kingdom'.[58]

Christian biography bears eloquent testimony to the values - and costs - of accepting this 'gift' or 'calling' to heterosexual celibacy (not only in the monastic vocation, but in missionary, pastoral and other callings also.)[59] One of the ways in which God's 'gift' and calling may be discerned is by the circumstances of a person's life and personality, environment and background. As a parallel, therefore, to the call to celibacy 'given' to those heterosexual 'eunuchs' who may well not have chosen it ('from birth', 'made so by men') as well as to those who voluntarily 'made themselves' such for the sake of the Kingdom, so the realisation by a person of his or her homosexual disposition may be understood as evidence of a calling from God to a life of celibacy, and the existence of the calling implies the presence of the gift.

As with heterosexual celibacy, its values - and its costs - are often great. In particular, the cost of relating as a sexual being without physical expression of sexual feelings is not to be minimised or denied. As Dr. Dominian says with reference to those who choose a vocation to the celibate religious life, after reference to the sustaining, healing and growth usually potentially present in marriage:

This sustaining, healing and growth of the human person needs to go on just as much in the single person, and a person entering the single state must possess characteristics in their personality which can compensate for the absence of an exclusive one-to-one relationship with its powerful capacity for sexual renewal. This means that single people far from denying their sexuality – whatever its intensity – accept it and make it a part of their conscious self.[60]

So likewise we would add, the celibate homosexual person needs to find ways of relating with others which promote growth, healing and affirmation. The Christian community should be the place where such ways can be found, and where such personal characteristics can be helped to grow.

To revert to our discussion of Smedes' third step of "accommodation": He now considers the moral standing of the homosexual person for whom neither change nor celibacy seem practicable options. Such a person, he says, is to develop an 'optimum morality' in this tragic situation, in which to live out his sexual life.[61] At this point Smedes appears cautiously to be conceding the permissibility of some homosexual behaviour as a lesser evil to promiscuity. But while 'an optimum morality' of a steady committed relationship may be judged preferable to a life of moral chaos, Smedes seems here to be crossing the absolute moral boundary which we have found in the biblical teaching. This is a point to which we shall need to give more discussion.

(b) Moral guidelines
We need first of all to remind ourselves that homosexual sin is not a more-than-equal sin. In the passages in which St Paul rules against active homosexual behaviour, he speaks of it alongside greediness and drunkenness (1 Cor 6.10), as well as alongside serious crimes. In the second place, we will be better able to assess the force of Smedes' conclusion by recalling the important distinction between the objective value of an act and the moral culpability of the agent. Although, in objective terms, homosexual acts are never morally good, the degree of blameworthiness of those involved in them is related to the circumstances surrounding them. Sherwin Bailey[62] suggests that a similar problem confronts us in the case of homosexual practices as confronts one seeking to allocate responsibility respectively to the burglar, the kleptomaniac, and the person who in desperate need takes what is not his own, while maintaining in each case the objective morality of the sinfulness of stealing. Homosexual acts are, from the biblical perspective, sinful acts, provided – as with all acts susceptible of moral evaluation – that they are free from external compulsion, and done with adequate knowledge in the agent. Unless it is claimed that the homosexual person is acting under a compulsion of such degree (extreme coercive threats, or temporary insanity for example) that he is relieved of all moral responsibility (in which case psychiatric help would normally in any case be necessary), he must be held to have freedom of choice not to engage in homosexual activity. But suppose any one particular act

114

is the expression of a very long-standing and deep seated set of mind and pattern of behaviour - such that moral blame should be apportioned much earlier in life than in this one act - can that person still be expected to refrain from homosexual behaviour? Psychiatrist John White believes so:

> No psychiatric help or 'cure' is needed to quit the practice. Go to a trustworthy friend, perhaps a Christian counsellor or prayer partner with whom you can be perfectly open and frank. Make a clean breast of your story. Talk with him. Pray with him. But so far as your practice of homosexuality is concerned, it must stop. Now. And if it has not yet started, then it must never be allowed to.
> I know what pain this might cause you. Straight friends find it hard to understand that you may deeply love someone of your own sex and that to break up with your lover will wound you in the same way as the breakup of any kind of illicit love wounds those involved. I know too that a period of sadness and even profound depression may follow the breakup.
> But do not fool yourself. You can do it. And you must...
> Whatever God may or may not do for you in the way of changing your sexual orientation, he can and will deliver you from any specific homosexual entanglement and from all homosexual activity.
> Your part is simply to quit. He does not promise freedom from grief or pain. But he does promise strength and consolation.[63]

That said, however, our attitudes to particular individual persons will rarely be identical. We do need to be able to distinguish between the homosexual acts of: those who are being awakened to sinfulness after a long period of sustained practice; those guilty of occasional lapses (The New Testament draws a distinction between those guilty of wilful sin and those "overtaken" in a trespass, Gal 6. 1); those who engage in deliberate acts in contravention of conscience; and those whose deliberate acts are in line with a conscience which has persuaded itself that homosexual activity can be morally good. In the last case two comments are appropriate: first that conscience binds, and for those who in sincere conscience do not judge themselves to be acting contrary to the will of God, that judgement of conscience must be respected - even if disagreed with. Second, however, conscience is by no means infallible. The New Testament itself shows how conscience can be 'seared' (1 Tim 4. 2), and it is an important part of the moral responsibility of Christian people to educate their conscience to the will of God. (As Sherwin Bailey notes, from the viewpoint of objective morality, the conduct of one who claims invincible ignorance is still at least in the area of material, if not formal sin.)[64]

To revert to Smedes' third point, therefore, we find ourselves needing to shift his 'optimum morality' over into a distinction that, though all homosexual acts alike are morally wrong, not all alike are morally blameworthy. His 'optimum morality' is based on the view that homosexual desires for some people have to find some form of physical expression. That view is not shared by the biblical authors (as we saw in chapter 4). The Christian pastor must certainly recognise the conflict for the homosexual which the practical problems of finding ways of dealing with his sexual urges creates for him (as also for some adolescent and other heterosexuals who are preoccupied with sexual concerns) – a conflict for which careful pastoral guidance is all too rare. But we need also to note that a homosexual person's intense sexual craving is very often related to relational starvation, and that more broadly based opportunities for friendships with both sexes can reduce the intensity of such physical desires.[65]

The Christian homophile struggling with the desire to give physical expression to his apparently irreversible inclinations needs, then, first of all to see his condition as a calling from God to a life of celibacy, and to recognise that such a calling implies the presence of the gift of celibacy. And then he needs to be encouraged to spread his relationships and develop friendships with both sexes. Furthermore, it is incumbent on him - as with us all - to maintain spiritual life and fellowship, and to use to the full the resources of confession, prayer, sacrament and spiritual nourishment in the Word of God.

It is essential to follow these statements with an acknowledgement that, while it may be comparatively easy to discuss morality objectively, for homosexual people it can be very difficult to live within its terms. Some homosexuals' situations may be a most complex vortex of difficult relationships, of emotional deprivation, of early trauma, and of present loneliness. The individual caught in such a vortex may be particularly prone to self-rejection, fear and distorted self-perception. Engagement in a homosexual act may not indeed initially have been a matter of will or desire, although a subsequent behaviour pattern may be. For such a person to achieve a moral life within biblical terms is difficult. Such difficulties are compounded, moreover, when, as all too often, the homosexual Christian finds himself in the setting of a Church which, rather than giving the utmost in support and strength, creates a judgemental attitude which merely magnifies loneliness and despair.

Smedes' option of an 'optimum morality' for the Christian homophile might not even have needed suggesting if there could be guaranteed for him a supportive context in which he could learn to affirm himself, accept the abnormality of his condition, be freed from the burden of false guilt, and learn to express his full nature (including his ability to relate as a sexual being but without specifically sexual acts) by spreading his relationships with his brothers and sisters in Christ.

As usual, C. S. Lewis's comments are most apt: the following quotations are from a letter by Lewis in response among other things to a question about the legitimacy for Christians of homosexual behaviour:

I will discuss your letter with those whom I think wise in Christ.

116

This is only an interim report. First, to map out the boundaries within which all discussion must go on, I take it for certain that the physical satisfaction of homosexual desires is sin. This leaves the homo. no worse off than any normal person who is, for whatever reason, prevented from marrying. Second, our speculations on the cause of the abnormality are not what matters and we must be content with ignorance. The disciples were not told why (in terms of efficient cause) the man was born blind (Jn IX. 1-3); only the final cause, that the works of God shd. be made manifest in him. This suggests that in homosexuality, as in every other tribulation, those works can be made manifest: i.e. that every disability conceals a vocation, if only we can find it, wh. will 'turn the necessity to glorious gain'. Of course, the first step must be to accept any privations wh., if so disabled, we can't lawfully get. The homo. has to accept sexual abstinence just as the poor man has to forego otherwise lawful pleasures because he wd. be unjust to his wife and children if he took them. That is merely a negative condition. What shd. the positive life of the homo. be? I wish I had a letter wh. a pious male homo., now dead, once wrote to me – but of course it was the sort of letter one takes care to destroy. He believed that his necessity could be turned to spiritual gain: that there were certain kinds of sympathy and understanding, a certain role which mere men and mere women cd, not give. ... Perhaps any homo. who humbly accepts his cross and puts himself under divine guidance will, however, be shown the way. I am sure that any attempt to evade it (e.g. by mock- or quasi-marriage with a member of one's own sex even if this does not lead to any carnal act) is the wrong way.....
All I have really said is that, like all other tribulations, it must be offered to God and His guidance how to use it must be sought.[66]

4. Concerning the wider Christian fellowship
The needs of the wider Christian fellowship are often as great and as urgent as those of the Christian homophile within it. They may be summarised under the headings 'repentance', 'education', and 'ministry'.

(a) Repentance
Richard Lovelace's prescription for a healthy church life in which Christian homophiles can be fully welcome members involves what he calls a 'double repentance'. Alongside his calling to practising Christian homosexuals to repentance for sin, and his urging of them to renounce their 'gay' lifestyle, he also urges repentance on the wider fellowship from its 'homophobic prejudices.'

Persons who are compulsively uneasy, fearful or filled with hatred when relating to persons involved in sexual sin, either homosexual or heterosexual, need a releasing work of the Holy Spirit, freeing their own sexual natures, building in them a sense of security which will permit them to express Christian

117

love while standing firm against impurity.[67]

Repentance involves change, and it is incumbent on the wider Christian fellowship to repent of attitudes of rejection, and work at being the fellowship of support in which the summoning of practising homosexuals to repentance and a change in their lifestyle in Christ's name can be made realistically in the context of warm and supportive charity, and not cold Pharisaic legalism. Although we have described the homosexual condition as 'learned', it is usually acquired involuntarily, and a recognition of this fact should provoke sympathetic and caring responses rather than moralistic abhorrence or legalistic coercion. We are not at liberty to urge the Christian homosexual to celibacy and to a spreading of his relationships, unless support for the former, and opportunities for the latter, are available in genuine love.

Martin Hallett, a former practising homosexual, now celibate and working as Counsellor for True Freedom Trust, believes 'that one of the most fundamental answers to homosexuality, and to many other problems (homosexuality is just one more result of the Fall), is for Christians to learn much more about truly fulfilling, loving relationships in Christ.' He continues:

> I long to see the Church as a really glorious manifestation
> of the Body of Christ, so that people, including homosexuals,
> will see the wonderful new life that the Lord Jesus offers, and
> His answer to all their problems displayed through His people.
> But the homosexual will remain beyond the reach of the Church
> as long as there are Christians, especially ministers and lay
> workers, who refuse to move out of their entrenched positions.[68]

(b) Education

> To leave up to one person in twenty with no other realistic
> option than self concealment is particularly unworthy of a
> church whose Lord and Master was ready to leave the
> ninety nine for the sake of the one.[69]

The heterosexual majority – many of whom are as unclear about their heterosexuality as any homosexual may be of his homosexuality – needs to be educated. Scanzoni and Mollenkott rightly criticise the unworthy 'stigma and stereotyping' attached to homosexually inclined brothers or sisters in Christ by some Christian fellowships.[70] The wider fellowships need to learn not only the facts about the homosexual condition, but also something of the pain and loneliness experienced by someone who discovers that his or her own preferences are homosexual. They need to learn the difficulties that surround the making of even 'ordinary' friendship relationships because of the difficulties of misunderstanding when the potential of less usual erotic elements are present. They need to learn to distinguish between an avowed and freely entered homosexual lifestyle, and occasional lapses into sin by those struggling with severe temptations. They need to approach sin in others not only with the Gospel of forgiveness, but through the eyes of Christ and not the Pharisee, and with constant awareness of the hypocrisy of speaking of sin in others with a beam in one's own eye.

Alongside 'Harbinger', the confidential counselling service for men and women homosexuals seeking Christian counsel of which Michael Hallett is Director, the True Freedom Trust has also established 'Chandler', a teaching ministry to churches and fellowships, seeking to provide teaching material for the education of Christian groups with a view to minimising the fears both of the Christian homophile and of his brothers and sisters in Christ.[71] This is a pattern that needs to be developed.

(c) Ministry
Part of the ministry of the Christian fellowship to Christian homophiles is to provide a context in which they can, if they wish, be relieved of the burden of secrecy, and know that they can share their particular needs and temptations among a group of accepting and supporting friends. Further than this, it is part of the responsibility of the whole Church, and of local congregations within it, to learn how to offer Christian counsel which will provide hope and opportunities of change for those struggling with homosexual needs. This ministry is no glib 'pray about it and all will be well'; it is an expert (in the sense of 'wisely experienced'), trained pastoral task involving the church's healing ministry, absolution,, education of consciences, spiritual sustenance, and counselling for change. It calls for a recovery of Practical theology and Pastoral coun-selling within our church. Such pastoral counselling with a homosexual person who is willing for his homosexual behaviour patterns to be changed might typically involve the pastor in establishing a close relat-ionship with the person concerned, whereby he may see him at first daily, then every other day, then weekly, and so on, each time checking on progress, affirming steps forward with joy, and exploring lapses back with compassion and hope. As with all particularly vulnerable people, a change in whose behaviour patterns can be felt to be deeply threatening to their whole personal identity, the pastor needs to invest a great deal of himself, his time and his gifts, into such caring support, prayer and counsel. It is no easy task, and cannot be undertaken lightly. It belongs within the context of a loving and supportive Christian Church.

The 'Chandler' teaching ministry of the True Freedom Trust offers training sessions and literature for the following purposes: 1) To help churches and Christian fellowships to understand the nature of homosex-uality. 2) To clarify the Scriptural position on this subject. 3) To set up, within church fellowships, a network of trained counsellors. 4) To link people who contact 'Harbinger' with a loving and understanding fellowship, who will 'build them up in the faith', and encourage them to minister to others. 5) To enable Christians with homosexual tendencies to be able to share their problems with others in their own church, without fear of rejection or misunderstanding.

119

Such aims could well be taken up much more widely.

(d) The ingredients of fellowship

It is appropriate to conclude with a summary of the ingredients of
Christian fellowship, as outlined in Eph 4. Christian fellowship entails
mutual acceptance (vv. 1-6). The first thing to be said of a homosexual
or heterosexual Christian is that he is a brother or sister in Christ.
Christian fellowship grows by mutual ministry (vv. 7-12). Each has
gifts that the other needs for spiritual growth; gifts of Christ's grace to
be offered and received. And Christian fellowship has as its goal
mutual progress 'to the unity of the faith and of the knowledge of the Son
of God, to mature manhood, to the measure of the stature of the fulness
of Christ' (vv. 13-14). This progress is achieved through 'speaking the
truth in love' (v. 15) - which involves calling one another back to the
pattern of life outlined in God's loving law appropriate for children of
God (v. 20), to a putting-off of the old nature and a putting-on of the new
(v. 22ff) - and through 'growing up into every way into him who is the
head'. (v. 15-16).

A healthy fellowship is characterised by the lives of those who 'truly
and earnestly repent of sin, are in love and charity with their neighbours
and intend to lead a new life following the commandments of God, and
walking in His holy ways.[72]

5. A Note on Society and Law

Following on from the above, 'it should not need arguing that people who
happen to have a homosexual orientation should be fully recognised as
human beings, and accorded all the usual privileges of citizenship' (as
Roger Moss puts it in Christians and Homosexuality,[73]) We cannot here
give space to a discussion of the issues of criminal law arising from the
Wolfenden Report, specifically whether or to what extent the criminal
law should be invoked in a 'paternalistic' role in the safeguarding of the
social cohesion which results from a particular shared morality.[74] But
the Christian does have a concern in social laws, stemming from his
conviction that, as Vidler put it, 'the first use of God's law is to pres-
erve human society in order and justice.' In line with the biblical
principles discussed in chapter 5 and the above discussion in this
chapter, such a concern will find expression in such ways as the
following: (i) the provision of a social environment which safeguards
and strengthens the fundamental Christian institutions of heterosexual
monogamous marriage, and the family, including a recognition of the
need to create learning environments which foster respect for sexual
complementarity and for the values of marriage and family;[75] (ii) the
rejection of legislation or practices which discriminate against homosexual persons on the grounds of their sexual orientation alone; (iii) the
maintenance of a social order which will dissuade from the affirmation
of homosexual practices as ever expressing what Curran called 'the full
meaning of human sexuality'; (iv) a caution with regard to laws involving
private sexual behaviour between consenting adults, which tend as
byproducts to increase opportunities for blackmail, invasion of privacy,

or restriction of reasonable freedom in personal decision-making, (within the limits of social and family stability, order and justice); (v) the protection of the young, immature and vulnerable, against seduction, or coercion into a homosexual lifestyle; (vi) the maintenance of socially accepted standards of public decency.

6. Some Ecclesiastical Questions

(1) Homosexual 'marriage'?
A (small?) minority of homosexual Christian couples in committed love relationship wish to ask the church to give its blessing to their union, and to witness an exchange of vows, and sometimes rings, in a formal service drawn up as a homosexual counterpart to heterosexual marriage. Indeed, the logic of any decision by the church to recognise some homosexual unions as falling within the will of God[76]would be for the Church to encourage and strengthen such unions with its recognition, blessing and support.

However, such a decision would have to be based on the view that of the many different aspects to heterosexual marriage in all its unitive and procreative possibilities, the 'relational' can be separated out as entirely unrelated to the establishment of family - a view which we have criticised earlier. Furthermore, from our conclusion concerning the sinfulness of homosexual behaviour (with varying degrees of blameworth-iness depending on its context), and from the normative nature of hetero-sexual 'one flesh' marriage, any suggestion of homosexual 'marriage' would not only be indefensible, but would significantly alter a Christian understanding of what the term 'marriage' means.

(2) Ordination
It seems clear that no one sensing a true call from God to the ordained ministry should be excluded from ordination on the grounds of homosex-ual orientation alone. Indeed the knowledge that celibate non-practising homosexuals were in positions of leadership in the Church could well serve to minimise some of the 'homophobia' still present in the church. From our earlier discussion of the sinfulness of homosexual acts, however, it is clear that a homosexually oriented person who engages in such acts with another, could no more be accepted for ordination than could a heterosexual person engaged in extra-marital sexual relationships.

Furthermore, in view of the (justified) public expectation of godliness of life in Christian leaders (supported, for example, by the qualifications laid down in the Pastoral Epistles, 1 Tim 3.1-13; Tit 1.7-9), those who are particularly prone to temptations to engage in homosexual or extra-marital sexual activity need - and should be enabled and encouraged to seek - particular help during ordination training, if not before. Oppor-tunities should indeed be made easily available for all ordinands to share problems of sexual orientation and temptation with a spiritual advisor (their Bishop, or Principal, for example). They should also be encour-aged to expect their spiritual and emotional maturity to be monitored during training, in view of the particular opportunities for sexual temptation which the parochial ministry can afford.

For all clergy, once ordained, the need for Christian fellowship in sustaining them in ministry is often keenly felt - the more so for those of homosexual orientation. The too common view that the clergy should make no close friends in the parish should be exposed for the damaging myth that it can be. All Christians need the fellowship, love and support of close Christian friends, and happy is the pastor who finds such within his own congregation. The homophile clergyman, in particular, would be greatly helped by the freedom to share the fact of his orientation and any problems associated with it with a small group of other mature Christians, and by the knowledge that he can depend on their love, prayer and support, and find emotional sustenance in relationship with them.

Some further words of Dr. Dominian, written with the needs of celibate (heterosexual, Catholic) priests in mind, are - it would seem - appropriate for this context also:

> If the sexual intimacy of marriage is not available to challenge and deepen self-awareness then clearly the life of the priest, both in training and later on, must have adequate substitutes, in other words strong emotional bonds with people of both sexes. This is easier to advocate than to arrange but within the love and security generated by Christian principles it should be possible to maintain close ties with people of one's own and with proper safeguards with the opposite sex, so that the necessary emotional encounter for personal growth can be found.

> The Church is still concerned with the risks that such intimate community life will involve. The answer clearly is that, if a man is not ready or capable of having close emotional relationships with people of his own sex and the opposite without being sexually involved, then he is not really pursuing the right vocation and the sooner this is discovered the better.[77]

(3) Church Discipline
If, as we believe from our examination of the biblical material, homosexual sexual behaviour (behaviour, not orientation) is invariably contrary to the will of God, the question of discipline within the Christian fellowship arises in connection with those involved in this particular sin. Indeed, the question arises with all sin - that is for all Christians at all times. The New Testament leaves no room for doubt that one of the marks of a healthy church is its concern for the purity of its corporate life.[78] Thus, says Paul, 'Let your manner of life be worthy of the Gospel of Christ ... be blameless and innocent, children of God without blemish in the midst of a crooked and perverse generation among whom you shine as lights in the world.' (Phil 1.27; 2.15).

But how is one Christian to react towards another Christian's sin? Jesus' words concerning the proper discrimination to be made between what is holy (Matt 7.6), life-giving (7.13-14) and good (7.15-20), and what is not, are set in the context of his words against the hypocrisy of censorious condemnation (7.1f.). Likewise, the apostle urges that 'you may be kind to one another, tenderhearted, forgiving one another, as God in Christ forgave you' (Eph 4.32; cf. Col 3.13). As Peter also says: 'Hold unfailing your love for one another, since love covers a multitude of sins' (1 Pe 4.8). However, love to another Christian includes the responsibility of encouraging him or her to live as accountable to God. Taking the apostle Paul as guide, we find him 'admonishing' his readers 'as beloved children' (1 Cor 4.14); proclaiming Christ' warning every man, and teaching every man in all wisdom, that we may present every man mature in Christ' (Col 1.28). The aim of his charge is love (1 Tim 1.5), and the task of 'teaching', 'admonishing', 'warning', he sees as part of the responsibility of each Christian towards their brothers and sisters. 'Warn him as a brother' (2 Thes 3.15); you are 'able to instruct one another' (Rom 15.14). As part of 'putting on love which binds everything together in perfect harmony' (Col 3.14), he urges 'Let the word of Christ dwell in you richly as you teach and admonish one another in all wisdom' (3.16). Such 'admonishing' will sometimes involve confronting a brother or sister with the fact of sin as well as making known the fact that sin can be forgiven. Part of this admonition belongs within the general preaching ministry, if this includes teaching about the character of God as revealed in his loving law. (Public teaching on the privileges and difficulties of celibacy, it is worth noting at this point, as a calling and gift, could also serve to encourage non-practising homosexuals within a congregation). But personal sin sometimes needs personal confrontation, and when against the person, our Lord's words are directly appropriate:

> If your brother sins against you, go and tell him his fault, between you and him alone. If he listens to you you have gained your brother. But if he does not listen, take one or two others along with you, that every word may be confirmed by the evidence of two or three witnesses. If he refuses to listen to them, tell it to the church; and if he refuses to listen even to the church, let him be to you as a Gentile and a tax collector. (Matt. 18. 15ff).

It is when a person's sin comes to the notice of the pastors of the church that the question of discipline, and sometimes exclusion from fellowship, becomes important, and difficult. Here, the New Testament gives us two ends to a spectrum within which each particular situation must be judged. In Gal 6. 1f, Paul teaches:

> Brethren, if a man is overtaken in any trespass, you who are spiritual should restore him in a spirit of gentleness. Look to yourself, lest you too be tempted.

The aim, as with the man 'punished' in 2 Cor 5.6-8, is to restore him to full membership through his penitence and forgiveness. In 1 Cor 5.1-7, however, the apostle is dealing with flagrant immorality. He reproves the church for tolerating the presence of a member guilty of incest, and then with apostolic authority excommunicates the offender, and calls on the church to associate themselves with this sentence. The object is the preservation of the whole community from infection (1 Cor 5.6), and the ultimate salvation of the offender (5.5). A similar separation from fellowship is appropriate for those guilty of other serious and unrepented sin, including the 'reviler' (1 Cor 5.11).

Whether or not a particular situation of sinful homosexual behaviour or of sinful 'homophobic' hostility, 'reviling' or recrimination, will call for either of these sorts of response from the local presbyters (for a member of the congregation), or from a Bishop (for a priest), would of course depend on the nature of the context, the needs of the persons and the fellowship concerned, and the degree of 'scandal', if any, involved. Any exercise of discipline for this or any other sin, needs to be handled carefully, for the good of the one so disciplined, and to avoid needless pain and greater scandal through inappropriate publicity. But Church discipline is no soft option. As E. J. Bicknell puts it in his comments on Article XXXIII:

> We need a new recognition of the practical holiness demanded from all members of the Body of Christ. This is not to fall into the Puritan error of limiting the Church to those who are actually holy. So long as a man is making an effort after holiness, even with many lapses, there is room for him in the Church. But there should be no place for those who do not even desire to live up to the standard of Christ and who actively set at naught Christian principles..... What is needed today is an awakening to the sense that churchmanship carries with it definite obligations.[9]

The primary point at issue is whether or not we love each other enough to call on each other to recognise our accountability to God, and whether or not we love God enough to ensure that the corporate life of our fellowship is 'worthy of the calling to which we have been called.'

NOTES

[1] J. Kleinig, 'Reflections on Homosexuality', Australian Journal of Christian Education, Papers 59, Sept. 1977, p. 32ff.
[2] C. E. Curran, Catholic Moral Theology in Dialogue, (University of Notre Dames Press, 1976 edition), p. 184 ff.
[3] Ibid., p. 219.
[4] Ibid.

⁵ See chapter 5 above.

⁶ J. Kleinig, op. cit.

⁷ Cf. Appendix 2 to chapter 2 of this Study.

⁸ A. C. Kinsey, et. al. Sexual Behaviour in the Human Male, p. 617.

⁹ Cf. here R. Moss, Christians and Homosexuality, (Paternoster, 1977), p. 15: 'At the heart of it, we are talking about something that happens in a limited area of the development of a person's personality, that is, to their characteristic, habitual set of attitudes, feelings and behaviours. What happens in this limited area of sexual orientation may be absorbed into a well-integrated character in such a way that it has no important repercussions on any other part of a homosexual person's life. At the other extreme, it may become the focal point – almost the creed – around which he builds his personality, and all the attitudes he has towards, and receives from, society.'

¹⁰ L. Scanzoni and V. R. Mollenkott, Is The Homosexual My Neighbour? (SCM 1978).

¹¹ C. S. Lewis, Prince Caspian (1951, Puffin edition 1973), p. 185.

¹² E. L. Mascall, 'Some Basic Considerations' in P. Moore ed. Man, Woman, and Priesthood, (SPCK, 1978) p. 20.

¹³ Cf. chapter 4.

¹⁴ Cf. Eph 2.8; 2 Cor 13.14; Rom 3.24; 2 Pe 3.18; Rom 5.15; 2 Cor 12.9; etc.

¹⁵ Eph 1.7, 19.

¹⁶ E.g. H. Bullinger, eighth sermon of Third Decade (1550); J. Calvin, Inst. II.7.6-14, (1559); the Lutheran Formula of Concord (1576).

¹⁷ A. R. Vidler, Christ's Strange Work (Longmans, Green & Co., 1944).

¹⁸ Ibid., p. 27.

¹⁹ Ibid., p. 38.

²⁰ Ibid., p. 42.

²¹ Ibid., p. 43.

²² J. Calvin, Inst. II. 7.12: 'The third and principal use, which pertains more closely to the proper purpose of the law, finds its place among believers in whose hearts the Spirit of God already lives and reigns... Here is the best instrument for them to learn more thoroughly each day the nature of the Lord's will to which they aspire, and to confirm them in the understanding of it... Again, because we need not only teaching but also exhortation, the servant of God will also avail himself of this benefit of the law: by frequent meditation upon it to be aroused to obedience, be strengthened in it, and be drawn back from the slippery path of transgression..... Doubtless David was referring to this use when he sang the praises of the law: 'The law of the Lord is spotless, converting souls;... the righteous acts of the Lord are right, rejoicing hearts; the precept of the Lord is clear, enlightening the eyes.' etc.

²³ Vidler, op. cit., p. 52.

²⁴ Though see O. R. Johnston, Christianity in a Collapsing Culture, (Paternoster, 1976).

²⁵ Vidler, op. cit., p. 66.

²⁶ This would include therefore both these offences in English law: buggery and gross indecency.

²⁷ D. S. Bailey ed. Sexual Offenders and Social Punishment, Church

Information Board, for C/E Moral Welfare Council, (1956), p. 77.
28 Jn. 4.24; 1 Jn 1.5; 1 Jn 4.16; Heb 12.29.
29 Quoting e.g. Ex 18.11; Deut. 10.14-17; 1 Chron 29.11-12;
Neh 9.6.; many ref. in the psalms and prophets; Ac. 4.24ff; 17.24-26;
Rom. 11.33-36; Rev 4.11 etc.
30 E.g. Jn 16.27; Rom 5.8; 1 Jn 3.1; 4.9ff. etc.
31 E.g. Eph 1.6-7; 2.7-9; Tit. 2.11; 3.4-7 etc.
32 E.g. Deut 5.10; Ps 136; Lk 6.35-6; 2 Pe 3.15; Rom 3.26; 1 Jn 1.9
etc.
33 E.g. Ex 15.11; 1 Sam 2.2; Isa 57.15; Hos. 11.9; Ac 3.14 etc.
34 R. Lovelace Homosexuality and the Church (Fleming H. Revell Co.,
Old Tappan, N.J., 1978), p. 132.
35 Vidler, op.cit., p. 36.
36 Lovelace, op.cit., p. 132.
37 Ibid., p. 133.
38 Cf. Rom 8.15; Rom 6.11; 2 Cor 5.17; Gal 4.5.
39 Col 3.9-10; 2 Cor 3.18; Eph 4.24. Cf. also R. Macaulay and
J. Barrs, Christianity with a Human Face (IVP 1979), 11ff.
40 Cf. Macaulay and Barrs, op.cit., p. 37.
41 So 2 Cor 3.18; Phil 2.12-13; 3.12ff; Eph 4.13, etc.
42 Cf. T. C. Hammond, In Understanding Be Men (IVF 1954⁵), p. 155.
43 Ibid., p. 157, referring to 1 Jn 2.1.
44 The expositions of D. M. Lloyd Jones are particularly helpful,
notably on Romans chapter 6: The New Man; Romans chapter 8.5-17:
The Sons of God; Ephesians 5.18-6.9: Life in the Spirit in Marriage, Home
and Work, (all published by Banner of Truth Trust).
45 I have derived much help from a paper 'Christian Counselling with
Homosexuals' by Stanley R. Strong, Professor in the Department of
Educational Psychology, the University of Nebraska-Lincoln, Lincoln,
Nebraska, USA.
46 1 Tim 6.12; 2 Tim 2.3; 4.7; Gal 5.16-24; Eph 6.10ff; Heb 12.1,4,12,
14; Rom 7.22-25 etc.
47 R. Lovelace, op.cit., p. 133.
48 E.g. F. MacNutt, O. P., Healing, (Ave Maria Press, Indiana 1974);
Agnes Sanford Healing Gifts of the Spirit (Arthur James 1966); Ruth
Carter Stapleton, The Gift of Inner Healing (1976); The Experience of
Inner Healing (1977); Michael Scanlan, Inner Healing; cf. also books by
Paul Tournier such as Guilt and Grace, a Psychological Study (Hodder
and Stoughton, 1962).
49 J. Dominian Cycles of Affirmation, (Darton, Longman and Todd,
1975), p. 89.
50 Cf. F. A. Schaeffer, True Spirituality (Hodder and Stoughton, 1972)
p. 149f.
51 E.g. R. Moss Christians and Homosexuality (Paternoster, 1977),
p. 40, referring to Ken Philpott The Third Sex? (Logos International,
1975) for example.
52 J. I. Packer, art. 'Temptation' in J. D. Douglas ed. The New
Bible Dictionary (IVF 1962), p. 1251.
53 R. Lovelace, op.cit., p. 131.
Ibid., p. 137.

[55] L. B. Smedes, Sex For Christians (Eerdmans, 1976)p. 64.

[56] Ibid., p. 70.

[57] Ibid., p. 72.

[58] Quoted from D. Hill, The Gospel of Matthew New Century Bible, (Oliphants, 1972), p. 281.

[59] Thus, for example, Henry Martyn's willingness, though not without pain, to forego marriage with his love for the sake of his missionary calling (C. E. Padwick Henry Martyn, SCM 1923, p. 113f.); and Richard Baxter's belief that a parochial clergyman would often be best single for the sake of his calling(The Reformed Pastor VIII (5) 2.)

[60] J. Dominian, Cycles of Affirmation, p. 69.

[61] Smedes, op.cit., p. 73.

[62] D. S. Bailey ed. Sexual Offenders and Social Punishment, p. 77.

[63] John White, Eros Defiled, (IVP 1977), p. 132f.

[64] D. S. Bailey, op.cit., p. 80f.

[65] One pastoral and practical book about sex is Michael Saward And So To Bed? first published by Logos International 1975; now by Grove Books, Bramcote. The practical question is also raised in R. Moss Christians and Homosexuality; cf. also M. Barker Homosexuality, Christian Medical Fellowship, 1975, p. 5. Cf. also Smedes op. cit.

[66] Quoted in S. Vanauken A Severe Mercy (Hodder, 1977), (Pbk 1979), p. 146f.

[67] R. Lovelace, op.cit., p. 129.

[68] Martin Hallett, 'The Christian and the Homosexual', Life of Faith March 1978.

[69] David Field, The Homosexual Way - A Christian Option? (Grove, 1976) p. 23.

[70] Scanzoni and Mollenkott, op.cit., p. 43ff.

[71] True Freedom Trust, P.O. Box 3, Wirral, Merseyside, L49 6NY. Tel. 051-678-9961. Another evangelical counselling service, staffed by F. Geoffrey Percival operates c/o Longfleet Vicarage, 60 Longfleet Road, Poole, Dorset; 020-13-77044.

[72] The invitation to Holy Communion, Book of Common Prayer.

[73] Op.cit., p. 16.

[74] E.g. the debate between Patrick (Lord) Devlin The Enforcement of Morals (OUP 1965) and H. L. A. Hart Law, Liberty and Morality (OUP 1963), and especially the interpretation and clarification of the debate by B. Mitchell Law, Morality and Religion in a Secular Society (OUP 1967).

[75] Cf. the editorial comments by W. E. Anderson and B. V. Hill 'Sexuality and Education' in Australian Journal of Christian Education, Papers 59, Sept 1977.

[76] The logic, also, of Smedes' 'optimum morality' which we discussed earlier.

[77] J. Dominian Cycles of Affirmation p. 107.

[78] Cf. e.g. F. A. Schaeffer The Church Before the Watching World (IVP, 1972) and especially The Church at the End of the Twentieth Century (Hodder edition, 1975).

[79] E. J. Bicknell A Theological Introduction to the Thirty-Nine Articles of the Church of England (Third edition revised by H. J. Carpenter, Longmans Green & Co. 1955), p. 318f.

DATE DUE

MAY 2 6 2006

DEMCO, INC. 38-2931